Prentice-Hall International, Inc., London
Prentice-Hall of Australia Pty. Limited, Sydney
Prentice-Hall Canada Inc., Toronto
Prentice-Hall Hispanoamericana, S.A., Mexico
Prentice-Hall of India Private Limited, New Delhi
Prentice-Hall of Japan, Inc., Tokyo
Prentice-Hall of Southeast Asia Pte. Ltd., Singapore
Whitehall Books Limited, Wellington, New Zealand
Editora Prentice-Hall do Brasil Ltda., Rio de Janeiro

HOURLY SELLING

Your Fast Track to Sales Success

CLINT DAWSON

A SPECTRUM BOOK

Prentice-Hall, Inc.
Englewood Cliffs, New Jersey 07632

Library of Congress Cataloging in Publication Data

Dawson, Clint.
   Hourly selling, your fast track to sales success.

   "A Spectrum Book"—T.p. verso.
   Bibliography: p.
   Includes index.
   1. Direct selling.   2. Time management.   I. Title.
HF5438.25.D39 1985   658.8'5   84-26448
ISBN 0-13-395013-1
ISBN 0-13-395005-0 (pbk.)

1 2 3 4 5 6 7 8 9 10

Cover design © 1985 by Jeannette Jacobs
Manufacturing buyer: Frank Grieco

ISBN 0-13-395013-1

ISBN 0-13-395005-0 {PBK.}

This book is available at a special discount when ordered in
bulk quantities. Contact Prentice-Hall, Inc., General
Publishing Division, Special Sales, Englewood Cliffs, N. J. 07632.

Contents

Preface

This book deals with time discipline for salespeople; it teaches them the necessity of balancing their business time with their family and leisure time. The book discusses the discipline problems encountered by salespeople and how they may be overcome through the use of the "hourly" system. It also analyzes the psychology of the salesperson. This book is not a manual on how to convince the customer; it is a salesperson's guide to staying realistically motivated from day to day. *Hourly Selling* explains how you can concentrate on selling without first having to worry about the "positive attitude" required by other sales techniques. It is a down-to-earth method of time discipline that is easy to follow. The hourly selling system forces you to work hard enough to become a successful salesperson, but it also requires you to take enough time off to be able to live a balanced life.

ACKNOWLEDGMENTS

Special thanks go to the following:

- My wife, Sharon, who spent many hours both typing and proofreading my manuscript and who, in addition, gave me much-needed moral support;
- My parents, Woodrow and Hilda Dawson, who taught me the values of independence and hard work—both of which are essentials in direct sales;
- Matt Donahue, who brought me into direct sales and who is committed to making sales a business, rather than just a "peddling" job;
- My fellow salespeople at Domestic Counselors, Inc., whose willingness to share selling ideas added a great deal of insight to my writing;
- Royal Prestige Products, whose nationwide network of distributors, professional sales conventions, management seminars, and publications has given me a wide range of ideas with which to compare my own.

1

*Introduction
to Hourly Selling*

Hourly Selling is not another theory of self-improvements based on some variation of Positive Mental Attitude (PMA). It does, however, assume that you have some knowledge of and are influenced by the principles of PMA. It also assumes that you are reasonably well trained in your particular sales field. *Hourly Selling* is not a sales manual or a book on how to deal with people. It is a book on how to deal with yourself. Hourly selling is a way to discipline your time to increase sales while living a more balanced life. The biggest enemies of most salespeople are not the customers, but themselves. Countless salespeople could greatly improve their sales if they had a foolproof way of disciplining their time. Hourly selling is just such a way.

The beauty of it is that it can be built around each salesperson's individual personality. No one has to get hyped up or leave his comfort zone to apply the principles of hourly selling!

You need to be familiar with PMA to understand what hourly selling is not. Any good sales organization will constantly train and emphasize the importance of looking positively at everything that happens to you in your job and your life in general. A person also should try to attend an occasional PMA rally or success seminar, many of which are frequently held in various cities across the country. These rallies usually feature big-name dynamic speakers. Self-help courses, such as those of Dale Carnegie, also contain a lot of positive attitude development. Anyone desiring self-improvement can seek further PMA influence from good books such as Zig Ziglar's *See You at the Top** or Norman Vincent Peale's *The Power of Positive Thinking*,† just to name two. Even sales conventions or local sales training meetings are like mini–PMA seminars.

If you have had that type of PMA influence, you have probably felt a positive enthusiasm from it. Why is it, then, that not everyone who is exposed to PMA comes out a complete success? Many professional speakers will admit that only a small percentage of the people who come to their

---

*Ziglar, Zig. *See You at the Top*. (New York: Putnam, 1982).
†Peale, Norman Vincent. *The Power of Positive Thinking*. (New York: Fawcett, 1978).

seminars will go to work and apply what they have learned. Most sales companies have to hire and train many persons before they find someone who will really apply his training. Just as you remember the positive feeling you got from a good seminar, you also probably remember how quickly that feeling vanished when you returned to the grueling reality of the sales field.

There are three categories of people who try sales. The first category is the one who turns into a success almost instantly. This person seems always to be naturally full of PMA and his impressive sales confirm it. Put this kind of person with any reasonably capable company and you will have a success. The second type of person who enters sales is the one who manages to apply enough PMA to be moderately successful but never becomes really great. The third type is the person who was turned on by the benefits of sales but who drops out shortly after starting. There is nothing anyone can do to help this person, who was simply lured by the independence and money potential in sales. This explains much of the failure rate in sales. Money and independence are a part of the free enterprise dream, and sales is the epitome of that dream. Many people at one time in their life have been lured by sales. Most of us have a relative who tried selling encyclopedias for two weeks. This third category of "dropouts" represents the majority of people entering sales, and they get weeded out quickly. When you discount this group of people, who should not have been in sales anyway, the failure rate of new salespeople is not nearly so depressing as one might think. No company has ever been able to devise a truly accurate way to separate these people from the others without actually hiring them. We simply have to give equal opportunity and training to all who seem positive and ambitious and let them go through the merciless weeding-out process themselves. I am not putting these people down, because they are probably well suited and needed for other professions. However, they are not needed in the sales profession.

Take away the large third category and we are left with the first and second categories. Let's look again at the first category. These people are the model successes of their business. They seem to have some kind of built-in time clock that always keeps them on course, making sure they are putting in plenty of time selling. That selling time results in impressive sales totals. They are truly the *good* salespeople. They are effective with people and put on a good sales call. Moreover, they always seem to be putting on *lots* of sales calls. They uncannily find the early-morning appointments and hidden leads that usually elude the rest of us. They also seem "luckier" than most, running into multiple sales and large packages. Just how do they do it? the rest of us ask. What mystical quality do they have? There is a lot to be learned from these *good* salespeople, and in this book I will refer to them frequently.

Since no theory can help the people in the third

category, and those in the first category do not need help, it is the second category that *Hourly Selling* can help. Another word for the second category is *average* or *mediocre*. It is almost a worse insult to be called mediocre than a failure. The *average* salesperson can be recognized only by his sales totals. He probably sounds just as positive as a *good* salesperson and has actually reached a certain degree of success. (Just surviving in a sales business proves that he has something on the ball.) While on a sales call, he is probably as effective with people as the *good* salesperson. However, he never seems to end up with anything above average for a yearly sales total. He says things such as, "If I could just discipline my time, I could be a great salesperson." He feels that he is actually a good salesperson who just does not work as much as the *good* salesperson, and he is right! The question is, "Why doesn't he?" Certainly he doesn't really want to dwell in mediocrity the rest of his life. It seems quite obvious that time discipline is his only real problem.

Remember when I mentioned that the first category of *good* salespeople seemed to have a built-in time clock that seemed to keep them naturally motivated? Well, unfortunately I was born without one, just as were all the other salespeople of that second category. With hourly selling I have, in effect, manufactured my own time clock to keep me on course. Because my sales have increased, I may have even fooled a few people into thinking that

I am a *good* salesperson. Little do they know that I am still my old mediocre self with only a makeshift time clock called hourly selling helping me out. The important thing is that it works! And if it works for me, it can work for other people like me.

There are thousands of direct-sales companies in the country. They typically have a few super-producers, with the remainder of the sales force far behind. Except for the superproducers, most salespeople represent the second category of person and can benefit from *Hourly Selling*.

2

*The Origin
of Hourly Selling*

As I finish writing this book, I am completing my sixteenth year of working in direct sales. In my business we sell specialized quality lines of china, stoneware, waterless cookware, and cutlery on a demonstration basis directly in the home. The distributorship I work with (Domestic Counselors Inc.; home office: Minneapolis, Minnesota) sells Royal Prestige Products (home office: Madison, Wisconsin). *Hourly Selling* actually evolved from a crisis point in my life that occurred in 1979. It is also based on my desire to be successful in business but to live a balanced life as well. What I mean is that besides working hard, I feel it is important to have time off for family, recreation, and keeping physically fit.

My crisis resulted from trying to expand my sales organization faster than I could actually afford to. I got myself into a vulnerable position, and when a few things took a bad turn I found my business in a serious financial crunch. I am sure that some of you in sales can identify with that kind of situation.

The good thing about that crisis is that it caused me to start analyzing how it had happened and how to prevent it from happening in the future. I analyzed my personal as well as my business life. I got into sales on a part-time basis while going to college. After my fourth year of college I became a full-time employee, and the company opened a branch office for me to run. That was really exciting. At twenty-one years of age I had my own office! My job, besides selling, was to hire, train, and motivate other salespeople. Within two years our yearly sales totaled $250,000, which at that time was a respectable job in our business. Good as well as bad years followed. In ten years more than 500 new salespeople were hired and trained through my office. Out of those people came many successes as well as failures.

We were constantly trying to discover what trait makes a good salesperson. We never did find a personality trait that could be identified prior to actually hiring the person. We found that introverts had as good a chance to succeed as extroverts. Total years of education made little difference. How positive or confident they sounded did not matter either. Even physical appearance had little effect. Anyone who has experienced a sizable cross section of salespeople would have to agree that no single personality type is exclusive to successful salespeople.

The only indicator that we ever came up with was that of a person's *desire level*. The people who make it in sales seem to have a greater desire to succeed than the general population. However, that desire level cannot be indicated by such a superficial thing as how ambitious they sound initially. It can be determined only *after* they have actually experienced sales for a while. By definition, the salespeople of the first and second categories must have that level of desire to survive in sales, or they would have quit right away and would be classified in the third category.

The *good* salespeople of that first category have the necessary level of desire, along with a seemingly natural way of disciplining their time to get the most out of their business. On the other hand, the people of the second category survive but often seem frustrated because they are falling far short of their potential. They just do not have a good handle on time discipline.

It should not come as a surprise that time discipline is a problem to so many salespeople. In almost any other job, time discipline is already taken care of. You have to be at work during certain hours, and if you don't show up you will probably be fired. A salesperson is in charge of his own time, which is a large responsibility. If a salesperson does not go to work he won't be fired, but he will in effect slowly fire himself by going broke.

My analysis of salespeople has been confirmed by many sources.

Royal Prestige Products, which Domestic Counselors Inc. sells in Minnesota, are also sold by other distributors similar to us throughout the nation. At national management seminars and sales conventions I have had the opportunity to compare ideas with hundreds of other managers and salespeople.

In addition to my own industry I have had numerous acquaintances and business associates in other direct-sales companies. They include real estate, insurance sales, Tupperware, Shaklee, Amway, vacuum cleaners, and business advertising and supply companies, just to name a few. Regardless of the product or service that is being sold, if it is direct sales, the success factor of each individual salesperson is his own time discipline.

If you are in a legitimate sales industry and are well trained, making sales to your customers should become rather routine once you gain some experience on the job. Your biggest enemy, as I have said before, is yourself. Since direct sales is making things happen, sales will occur only in proportion to the time you spend pursuing them. If you allow your attitude or unexpected interruptions to decrease the time you spend selling, your sales will suffer. Once again, the common denominator in making any direct sales is time discipline.

What motivates and qualifies me most to promote *Hourly Selling* is my own sales performance, or rather the lack of it. During my first ten years in sales my personal sales were average. They were certainly always less than I wanted them to be. Sure, I had management responsibilities, but I let them interfere too much with my selling time. During my business crisis I put together *Hourly Selling* and have since then more than tripled my sales! I have been consistently in the top 5 to 10 percent of the company nationally. Imagine what it was like, after being in a rut of mediocre sales for ten years, to accomplish a change like that. Moreover, I did it without changing my style or personality. I just applied my hourly selling principles!

Also, because my selling time was disciplined and predetermined I have been able to live a more balanced life, blending work with enjoyable time off. I recall going to opposite extremes in previous years of my life. For periods of time I would overwork. When business is good and you are enthusiastic, it is easy to become a workaholic. But you eventually pay a price for that. Your family and personal sanity suffer. Many people reach a burnout stage at some point. The other extreme is taking too much time off, which can be relaxing for a while, but it eventually results in loss of goals and low self-esteem, not to mention financial vulnerability. Hourly selling allows for but simultaneously guards against those pitfalls.

Hourly selling does require a commitment on your part, but it offers very specific practical guidelines. It is something that, once you have the desire to change, you can really set your mind to. All of the positive-attitude teachings tell you what you should be doing, but they do not tell you how to do it day by day and hour by hour. The worst torture for a salesperson is to be exposed to PMA but to realize later that he is failing to apply what he has learned. The practical guidelines of *Hourly Selling* spell out exactly how to apply its principles.

3

A Definition of Hourly Selling

It is important to understand what hourly selling will or will not do for you. It is not a spectacular cure-all for ailing sales. It will, if applied without deviation over the long haul, provide you with enough business so that you will receive a very good income for your time. That is the only real definite benefit that I can guarantee.

Hourly selling is, very simply, setting a predetermined number of hours that you are going to spend on selling each week and never deviating from it, regardless of circumstances or interruptions. You never put in more or fewer hours than your predetermined amount.

The benefits from this approach to time discipline are intangible as well as tangible. It is directed at peace of mind as well as at making consistent sales.

Hourly selling requires effort. It is not easy, but it is simple, and when something is simple, it becomes easier. It requires a commitment on your part. Furthermore, it requires you to be more honest with yourself than you ever dreamed. It will give you a fresh, realistic, attainable goal every week. It requires very little enthusiasm and almost no positive mental attitude. I have almost stopped believing in PMA (Positive Mental Attitude). I have really started to believe in PMA (Positive Mental Action)! You go out selling first and get positive later. You actually put the cart before the horse, but to your amazement, the cart will start pulling the horse! Hourly selling is a refreshingly opposite approach to the usual "fire-'em-up-with-positive-attitude" kind of motivation. The basic premise starts from a hard, cold, almost negative standpoint and works its way into something very solidly positive: good consistent sales. You will find yourself acting out all the positive things other people are still only talking about. Never again will you have to get fired up or psyched up in order to go out selling. How many times have we heard ourselves say, "Well, I guess it's about time to get fired up and go out selling"? The fallacy of this approach is that it implies that if you can't get motivated or fired up, you won't be able to sell.

Let's assume that for today you do manage to get fired up but do not happen to get an order.

Tomorrow, when you try to fire up, your sub-conscious will be reminding you that yesterday you went through the effort of getting motivated but did not get any results. The same mental devastation comes when you get sales that later cancel, thereby punishing your well-intended motivation efforts.

This is not to say that every time you go selling you will get negative results. However, in a typical work week there are many negatives mixed in with the good sales we get—things like missed sales, cancellations, broken appointments, leads not home, bad weather, people who hate salespeople, and so on. Let us compare these negatives with those of someone with a "normal" job—say, a carpenter. Here are some negatives he may put up with: fourteen bent nails, wall in wrong place, eight boards cut too short, hammer broke, ran out of window frames. He probably looks at these as only routine frustrations of his job and would continue to work because he will get paid anyway, and the house will still get built. That is the way hourly selling enables you to view the negatives in your job of selling. You are going to put in your weekly quota of hours because you know that you will get enough good business on the average to earn your pay, and your goal of building a respectable sales total will eventually be realized.

As I now propose a new trend in sales motivation, there has already begun a new trend in how products are being sold to the consumer. An excellent book on that subject is *How to Sell in the*

1980s by Robert Montgomery.* It deals with the "participative" style of selling, which has the prospect doing more of the talking and the salesperson doing more of the listening. It replaces the canned sales pitch with the salesperson asking the proper questions to discover the prospect's real needs and desires. It personalizes the sales call.

Over the years people have tired of the old-fashioned, hyped-up, product-pushing type of sales. I think of this whenever I see a television commercial from the 1950s or 1960s. They are artificially professional and product-pushy compared with today's commercials. Advertisers today often use down-to-earth people and humor to get you to remember them. It is an attempt to personalize the commercial. Of course, television is very limited as to how personalized it can become.

There is a growing acceptance of home sales in our society today. It is, by definition, very personalized. It is something people crave in our increasingly technological world. The more people do business with automated tellers, computers, and drive-up businesses, the more refreshed they are when a good salesperson stops in and takes the time to care about how they feel.

It has been said that professional salespeople are master psychologists. They can adapt to any person of any educational or income level in any situation. They can draw out their prospect's true

---

*Montgomery, Robert L. *How to Sell in the 1980s.* (Englewood Cliffs, N.J.: Prentice-Hall, 1980).

feelings and quickly gain an understanding of what ideas he will react favorably to. Within the short time of a single sales call they can bring the prospect into their confidence and sell him hundreds of dollars' worth of merchandise. That can be done only with a professional, but low-key and personal, approach. On many occasions people have followed me out to my car to thank me and tell me that I made them feel comfortable and did not act like the "typical salesman."

There is, however, still a missing factor that is needed to succeed in sales. It is the salesperson's time discipline. A salesperson can have the best products and the best training and be a so-called master psychologist, but he can still fail if he does not discipline himself to get out and work. This is where hourly selling comes in. You see, hourly selling deals with the psychology of the salesperson. It analyzes the master psychologist. What makes him tick? What causes the failure or success of the salesperson?

There is a tremendous vacuum in sales motivation methods today. Just as the consumer has tired of the hyped-up hard sell, salespeople are growing weary of the single-minded "fire-'em-up-with-positive-attitude" type of motivation. Positive-attitude development is essential, especially for new salespeople. However, after a time in sales many people realize that there is a big gap between the motivational speakers they listen to and what actually happens to them on a day-to-day basis in the sales field. Hourly selling fills that gap. It allows the salesperson to be human. It basically says that it is okay to be lazy or negative at times. In fact, it even plans on it. It allows for all of the negative feeling we have while selling, but conquers them through the mechanics and guidelines spelled out in this book.

On several occasions I have been asked to give talks on my hourly selling at company seminars. At a seminar a couple years ago we had an industrial psychologist (Albert Lipp of Minneapolis) as a guest speaker. He heard my talk because I was up to speak before him. Afterwards I told him I was thinking of writing a book on it, and he said it should be "dynamite" because it is built around each individual salesperson.

Hourly selling is easy to identify with. It is something for the average person. It is a way to improve without a drastic change in personality. In some of my talks I have fun talking about how I have made selling boring. I jokingly refer to myself as the Tommy Newsom of the sales industry.

It is fun to get people's attention by saying a few controversial things like: "You don't need to be positive, you need very little enthusiasm—no goals, no ambitions, just hourly selling." But I am living proof that it works! Hourly Selling doesn't push people to be number one, but it does give them a way to improve and balance work with leisure in a rational manner.

I am also, as the author of the idea, someone that people can identify with. I am not an international selling superstar. I am a person whose sales were barely adequate for many years and who nearly went broke because of a lack of time discipline. However, with my hourly selling concept I more than tripled my sales and have made my business very profitable. I am not number one, but now I am always in the respected top 5 to 10 percent of the company, which includes several thousand salespeople. Furthermore, hourly selling lets me have my time off guilt free, which also makes it easy for people to identify with. In talking with spouses of our salespeople I find that they quickly pick up on hourly selling. They often are either disgusted that their spouses are not motivated to work enough or bitter because they are "always out selling." Hourly selling solves those problems because it states that taking time off is as important as forcing yourself to work.

The time has come for a new approach to sales motivation. As the field of home sales becomes more legitimate (thanks to some consumer protection laws) and is accepted in our society as a personalized way of buying, increasing numbers of people will make their careers in sales. *Hourly Selling* is directed at that stable career person.

Hourly selling is 1 percent theory and 99 percent practical application. The theory is extremely simple: If you put in a given amount of hours each week, you will get some sales. However, it does get more complicated and involved as we get into the mechanics of it. The theory provides that whenever you go selling you may choose from quite a variety of activities that may be justified as selling time.

You may be appalled at some of the things I somehow construe as selling time. Unless you fully understand the reasoning behind each selling activity, you may become disillusioned with it during a sales slump. That's right, a sales slump! Hourly selling does not guarantee against a sales slump, it only guarantees against an effort slump. However, if you have no effort slumps, your sales slumps will be fewer and shorter. When I get into all the technical definitions of selling time, I will go to some length to explain how I justify each because you must really believe in them. There will probably be times when this whole thing seems corny and over-technical, but the technicalities are what make this plan work because there is a lot of reasoning behind each one. With this in mind, let's proceed with the practical application of hourly selling.

4

Nowhere Else to Go

Let us start from a very basic, humble standpoint. Almost everyone needs to work for a living. If you quit your sales job, will you have to look for another job? Unless you have some means of obtaining food, clothing, and shelter without earning money, you will have to. Besides the things we need are the things we want: nicer homes and cars, and money for recreation, traveling, and financial security in general. Anyone who has a family will attest to the fact that it takes a lot of money just to live comfortably. If you have higher financial and business goals, they will require even more money.

If you did get another job, how many hours would you be required to work? In our society a forty-hour work week is presently considered a basic full-time job. In blue-collar work, anything over forty hours is considered overtime. In white-collar employment, forty hours is still considered basic full time, but anyone who moves up into any type of managerial or executive level will easily put in from forty-five to sixty hours a week. In other words, if you want a basic full-time job that will provide you a comfortable living, you will be working at least forty hours per week. If you have higher business or financial goals, you may work up to sixty hours per week. Very few salespeople put in an honest work week.

The key phrase there is *honest work week.* Many salespeople confuse being *at work* with *work.* Oftentimes salespeople have an office to go to for meetings and to make phone calls from. The association and support obtained from other salespeople around the office can be important. However, it can easily become a crutch. It can feel so good to sit around the office and socialize or do some miscellaneous paperwork that you do not notice how little actual productive work is getting done. If a salesperson hangs around the office for a total of twenty hours in a week and spends another twenty hours out selling, he did not work forty hours that week. He was only productive for the twenty hours he was out selling. Subconsciously, though, the salesperson tells himself that he worked the entire forty hours because that is the total time he was "at work."

Hourly selling will guard against that because it has definitions of what is or is not selling time. If a salesperson quit sales and went to work at a regular job, his employer would certainly be sure he was working at his assigned job for the entire week, instead of idly hanging around part of the time. So if a salesperson quits his job, he really has nowhere else to go to make a living on fewer hours of work. This may seem like a negative approach, but it will help you make a serious time commitment to your sales business.

5

*Setting
Your Hours*

Since there is nowhere else to go for fewer hours, how about considering a basic forty-hour work week with your sales job? If you have to put in forty hours of selling time as well, it won't be better than other jobs in that respect, but it won't be worse either, and it will be a lot more profitable!

Hourly Selling does not dictate how many selling hours you should put in. It only says that you should calculate and predetermine them based on your financial and personal time goals. The decision of how much you are going to work is made rationally, ahead of time, rather than in the middle of the excitement or frustration of a week.

Let us say a salesperson is having a really big week by Wednesday. Depending on the individual, two pitfalls can occur. One is to ease off for the rest of the week. The salesperson gets overconfident and subconsciously tells himself he is so smooth that he does not have to work very hard to get sales. What he neglects are the next week's accumulating leads. Also, what if those sales later cancel? Once time is taken off it can never be recaptured. The other pitfall is to work too much because of the excitement. It is easy for him to get so greedy that not enough time is taken off.

On the other hand, let us say that by midweek a salesperson has no sales. Again, depending on the individual, two pitfalls are likely. Out of frustration and self-pity the salesperson may not work much more. The other extreme is to take it as a challenge and to work too much to prove to himself and others that he cannot be discouraged. That is probably the better of the two reactions, but it still neglects having the proper time off away from the hassles of the business.

If you work for someone else, you have plenty of structure in your job. They will tell you where, when, and what to do. In direct sales, you work for yourself. Your conscience is your only guide as to when, where, and how much to work. Salespeople need a definition of when they *should* feel guilty if they are not working. Conversely, they also need a definition of when they *should not* feel guilty if they are not working. When one of our promising salesmen quit I asked him why. He replied, "I can't take the pressure." I asked him, "What pressure?" He said, "Whenever I take time off I feel like I should be out selling." He had not developed a concept of how to take time off. In order to not feel guilty, he had to be working all the time. That would drive most of us crazy.

The opposite problem is that most of us justify too much time off. By nature, most salespeople are not fond of paperwork. It can be very fatiguing. If you put in an afternoon of paperwork and three hours of selling time in the evening, you can probably justify a day's work based on how tired you feel. But was it really an *effective* day's work? Unless you keep track of the time you spent selling, you probably are fooling yourself as to actual productive time. A common justification of time off is "a big week." With hourly selling, you never fall into that trap. Another justification is a "bad week." You feel sorry for yourself and become depressed. Once again you justify pampering yourself. With hourly selling, you never fall into that trap either. A person using hourly selling has only one clearly defined goal each week: To put in his predetermined hours.

Some people use other measures to determine how much effort is enough. One way is to require a certain volume of sales from oneself before quitting each week. Another is a set number of appointments. Again, the select *good* salespeople seem to be the only ones this works for. If you have been using volume or appointments as a guideline and your sales are only average, you may as well admit it isn't working very well for you.

Using a certain volume of sales as a guideline

has two distinct disadvantages. First of all, let's say you happen to really get hot and sell a lot during the first half of the week. Because your volume is high, you may have a tendency to ease up too much. Think of the *good* salespeople you know: They keep on working each week no matter how well they are doing. Hourly selling will keep you working too because your goal is not sales achieved, but hours put in. You are forced to imitate the *good* salesperson's methods. The other disadvantage is the week that you do manage to put in an honest work effort but get few results. That certainly can happen. Maybe you are just having a bad streak or something. However, if you require a certain volume from yourself, you might have to work eighty hours to achieve it. That will only make you bitter and exhausted the following week. Hourly selling always lets you have time off even if you do not get your sales in a given week. A reasonable amount of time off assures that you will be fresh for the next week.

Using a set number of appointments as a guideline is one step better but has the same disadvantages as using volume. It is possible to put in a full work effort in a given week and still not get lots of appointments. However, it is *impossible* to put in forty hours of selling time in a given week and not get forty hours of selling time out of that week! In other words, *you will never fail to attain your goal in any week.* You may have to strain and plan in order to get in your hours, but it is no more complicated than that. All you have to do is fill up your hours with anything that can be considered selling time.

Ever get into one of those disgusting unmotivated moods? I am not sure if it is physical, psychological, or both, but sometimes a salesperson just does not feel like selling. If that happens, pick something that is easy to do. Maybe just go out and check for new leads. Take lots of time to write them down and keep them for another day when you feel better. If you did that for an entire day, you probably would accumulate lots of places to go. What usually happens after an hour or so of that, however, is this: You get into the mood to start working harder! The most common feeling of those unmotivated moods is that a salesperson does not feel like talking to people. The chain of logic is that because selling involves talking, if he is not in the mood to talk to anyone, he may as well not work. Hourly selling allows that kind of thing to happen to you, and you can still get something accomplished.

The key is to *be as comfortable as possible during all of your selling time.* You can pamper yourself with any type of selling activity you wish. If you have any sales incentive at all, you will find the motivation to give those appointments when the time comes. If you feel comfortable with your job, you will do better and be happier over the long haul. A content salesperson, who is not constantly in a hurry to get an instant sale, is a much better salesperson.

You also get a feeling of being in more control of your time. Your leads have to look during *your* selling hours. If they break an appointment, you should not be too offended. There is more work to be done during that time anyway. Ever had a hot lead at 9:30 A.M. on Saturday? You had worked a full week and deserved a weekend off, but you lined it up anyway because it sounded so good. When you went over there, however, they were not there. You probably went home rather disappointed. Now, if something like that happens to you, just plan on working for a couple of hours on that Saturday. That way you can subtract that time during the week, thus lightening your work load before next Saturday. If the prospect is not there, just go checking for new leads or something for those two hours.

The only catch to hourly selling is that once you set your number of hours, you must *never, ever* fail to get them in. Even if you have to work all weekend to do it you must get them in, or else you are not, by definition, on an hourly selling system. Remember, hourly selling will help you only if you are willing to do your part. The nice thing is that you need not feel under any immediate pressure to get a sale, and that is what makes the hours seem more feasible.

You will learn to scrutinize what things you will allow to delay your selling time. Each hour you waste during the week will cause you to work that much longer at the end of the week. You will only spend time on important office work, which will actually make you a better businessperson in the long run. You will also limit unnecessary socializing around the office or elsewhere. People will understand and ultimately respect that you are on an hourly system. Just say, "It's time for me to get some selling time in" and leave.

If you have so many delays in a given week that you absolutely cannot get your time in, your only option is to declare some vacation time, which will be covered more in a later chapter. On the other hand, if you work really hard you might be able to get all of your hours in in three or four days and earn yourself a long weekend off! The word "earn" is the key. Once your hours are in you have done your part and you can forget about selling until next week without an ounce of guilt.

Not only can you quit after your hours are in, you *must* quit. In order for hourly selling to accomplish its purpose, you cannot exceed your hours. The most you should ever exceed your hours is if you are in an appointment and you run a little late. However, try to schedule your time so that does not happen. If you are near the end of your hourly quota for the week with, let's say, less than an hour to go, work that hour, but be careful not to put on any sales calls. If you get in on a sales call, it can easily run over your hourly quota for the week, which must not happen.

Any salesperson with more than an ounce of sales instinct will cringe while reading that last paragraph. What kind of an idiot wrote this book anyway? Actually advising salespeople *not* to put on a sales call! Wait! Before you dip this book in gasoline and touch a match to it, please hear me out. Please read the entire book! (It is not that long anyway.)

There are numerous and varied psychological reasonings that make up hourly selling. Remember, hourly selling analyzes the salesperson. Hopefully, as you proceed through this book the logic of hourly selling will start to make sense and you will see that there is deeper, yet down-to-earth, thinking involved in it. This is not a "go-get-'em-and-make-a-million-dollars-in-a-week" kind of book. To write a book on keeping yourself positive and successful with PMA and belief in yourself would border on plagiarizing ideas, if not actual works, that have been already published.

As I said earlier, familiarity with and exposure to PMA are necessary. There are many fine books on the subject as well as courses, seminars, and rallies like those mentioned in chapter one. Most sales companies have absorbed and incorporated information from those sources into their sales training. In fact, a sales firm that does not include some positive attitude development in its training and motivation is way behind the times.

Hourly selling is ahead of the times. It is a new and realistic approach that gets right to the heart of the salesperson's actual feelings and actions. Of all the sales motivation techniques I have been exposed to in sixteen years of direct sales, I cannot think of a single source that spells out day-to-day applications of your selling time. A salesperson wishing for self-improvement will wisely seek out positive sales motivation through seminars, books, tapes, or company sales meetings. The result will almost always be increased enthusiasm and a desire to work harder and sell more. The problem lies in transferring that desire to the realities of day-to-day selling. There is a big gap between having a desire to succeed and actually applying that desire to the sales field for a significant period of time. Hourly selling is the approach that will bridge that gap. Once you have the desire to make a commitment to your sales job, the rules and guidelines of *Hourly Selling* will give you actual methods to achieve your long-term goals. I hesitate to call *Hourly Selling* a type of sales motivation because that carries with it the connotation that you will be all enthused and fired up when you get done reading it. Actually, I hope you are not *too* motivated after reading this book. The higher your level of excitement, the farther it will have to come down when you get back to the rejections and other negative factors a salesperson must deal with in a typical work week. Also, what about those lazy or negative moods you may get into from time to time? I don't care how motivated you may be at a given meeting or seminar, you will not stay that positive all the time. If you say you do not have those negative or lazy feelings, you are either a *good* salesperson of that first category or are lying to yourself and everyone else.

Let us not refer to hourly selling as "sales

motivation." Let us call it an "approach" to sales motivation. A new approach, a unique if not unorthodox approach, a thinking approach, a psychological approach, a working approach, a career approach...certainly a realistic approach.

When we are laboring through the details, bear with me. When my ideas seem to contradict everything you have ever learned, keep an open mind. When *Hourly Selling* is analyzing, think with me and analyze how all the details and guidelines have a greater purpose, that purpose being to increase your sales through inner motivation plus being able to balance your work and leisure time.

The things done while selling "hourly" are based on what a salesperson *actually* does, not on what he *should* do. Many of us who have been sales managers are guilty of ignoring what a salesperson actually does with his time. We only talk about what he should do. We say, "Why teach them any bad habits. They will learn enough on their own." That statement has validity, especially with newly hired salespeople. However, the longer people work in sales, the more they realize that they do not always follow good work habits. Furthermore, they realize that it is possible to survive in sales even with a few bad habits, but few people, especially managers, will admit it.

Well, Hourly Selling admits it. In fact, it meets the bad habits head on. It lets us be human. It allows us to both keep our good habits and get some use-fulness out of our bad habits. When you stretch the rules of hourly selling to the limit you get the feeling you are getting by with goofing off. As long as you remain within the guidelines, which will be outlined in the following chapters, you are not cheating. You are just using hourly selling to cater to your selfish or lazy or negative mood at the time. The rules are relaxed enough to give you that "goofing-off" feeling, but stringent enough so that you will get something done. Most importantly, they let you keep "putting your hours in" until your mood improves.

I do not want you to be ultra-motivated after reading this book, but I do want you to be convinced; convinced that it is a down-to-earth selling approach that will give you a feeling of stability in addition to increased sales. I also hope you realize that hourly selling can be adapted to your specific business. It can be done without drastic changes in your attitude or selling style. It will require you to make a serious effort commitment to fulfill your hourly quota each week, which will be the hardest part, but if you are not willing to make a time commitment, I question how strong your desire to succeed is. Remember, as Chapter 4 points out, you have nowhere else to go as a salesperson anyway.

ONLY A JOB

Direct sales is only a job to me. I hope you realize that I do not really mean that, but it is the premise from which I formulated the idea of hourly selling. You see, even after direct sales is stripped of all its positive hype, it is still a worthwhile job. Strip away all of the talk about the opportunity, the independence, the rags-to-riches stories, the recognition, trophies, awards, and accompanying excitement— all of those things we talk about to draw people into sales. Even with all of that taken away, direct sales can still be a profitable and enjoyable career.

A few years ago, when my business was in the deepest part of its financial crisis, I became so bitter and cynical that I rejected all of the positive slogans about sales that I had heard and that I myself had professed for many years. I had gotten myself thousands of dollars into the hole. It is amazing how fast business debts can add up. Add that to a person's constant need to earn a living on a monthly basis and the financial burden can become enormous. My desire to expand my sales organization and be super-successful had caused me to spend money and take chances that I could not really afford. What made me especially vulnerable was that I was neglecting my own personal sales, which of course is where I can make full profit. I simply was not disciplining my time to get out selling. Instead of me running the business, the business was running me. The desire to succeed without a hard-nosed commitment to self-discipline can be a dangerous combination.

For a while I literally faced financial ruin. Many times I mentally quit the business. "Why not just fold up the business and go get a regular job and live a normal life?" was a question that crossed my mind.

Why didn't I quit? There are actually several reasons. I suppose pride had a lot to do with it. I just hated the thought of not trying to right the wrongs. My lack of time discipline and its consequences were staring me in the face. The idea of hourly selling was born from that humiliation and self-analysis. I immediately started selling hourly. Hourly selling was a way to immediately begin righting the wrongs. For several years I was to be hassled by the financial situation I had caused, but by selling hourly week after week I was steadily rebuilding myself. My personal sales doubled, then they tripled. My excitement about a new selling approach was growing! Regardless of the financial hassles I had to endure, I knew that I now had a system that would make my business profitable. I could see that even if sales was "only a job," it could still be a great career. When thoughts of getting a "normal" job crossed my mind, I realized that I would have to work at least forty hours per week, and the most horrifying part was that I would not be able to be my own boss. Since I knew I would be working at a job anyway, I decided that it would not be the worst thing to put those hours in at my present sales job, especially now that I had found a way to make it very profitable. I also realized that sales was the only field in which I could earn the extra money necessary to pay off past business debts, thereby righting the wrongs that I was to blame for. The business that nearly caused me to go broke turned out to be the same business that I rebuilt myself in. Interesting, isn't it? The *business* itself did not cause anything. How I *used* the business is what finally made it stable and profitable. The method that accomplished that is called hourly selling.

For a long time my increased commissions went to paying off past business debts. It took a few years because I still had to keep up with current business expenses and support my family, but the excitement of a new selling system kept me going. This new system did not require me to be dependent on any external source of motivation to sell; all it required was a commitment to work.

I could also see how much extra money I would have once my past mistakes were paid for. That vision kept me going when I was down and enabled me to overcome incredible odds.

Other people quickly saw a change in me when I started selling hourly. Most importantly was the president of our distributorship, Matt Donahue. I must give credit here where credit is due. His belief in me through financial backing kept me afloat during the worst of my crisis, and I will be forever grateful.

It was interesting that after just a few weeks of hourly selling Matt could see that I had changed. He is a self-made multimillionaire, and he is not an easy man to impress. That is how quickly applying the principles of hourly selling can produce positive changes in a salesperson's performance.

As I started selling myself out of the hole hourly, I knew it would be a long-term recovery. I had to work very hard because of the financial pressures, but at the same time I had to allow myself some time off so I could endure the work over a long period of time. In other words, I had to pace myself. Thus came the hourly selling system's emphasis on taking time off. If any salesperson needs a sum of money fast, he can work extra hard for a few weeks or months to get it. That is definitely a benefit of the independence of sales. However, if you are going to sell over a longer period of time, it is a mistake to ignore your personal life just for the sake of money. I know some salespeople whose sales fluctuate in proprtion to their need for money. They goof off until they are out of money, then they become workaholics until they earn enough money, and then they goof off again and the cycle goes on and on. Clearly, they have no control of either their business or personal time.

I will admit that there were times when I had to force myself to quit at the end of the week when my hourly quota was fulfilled. When you need the money, it is tempting to never let up, but the physical and mental consequences of that are obvious. Even though rebuilding was unpleasant, I can look back and honestly say that I lived a reasonably balanced life throughout the entire experience. It was during that time that it occurred to me that hourly selling would be a good system even if a person were not in a business crisis. It is also a way for me to ensure that I will never make the same mistakes again.

I also started to believe that a book on hourly selling could help keep other salespeople from making the same mistakes that I made. *Hourly Selling* is very close to my heart because I had to learn the hard way. As the saying goes, the school of experience is the best teacher, but the tuition can be prohibitive. Hopefully, you can benefit from hourly selling without learning the way I had to.

Selling is a unique business opportunity that carries with it many responsibilities. You will be able to handle those responsibilities much more easily if you treat it as a job and apply yourself accordingly.

I have so conditioned myself to view selling as a regular job that I have almost developed a bored attitude towards it. Imagine that! Selling being boring! That is exciting! What an accomplishment! Selling is usually anything but boring. It can be very exciting, frustrating, or depressing, but it is almost never boring. And that is the problem with sales. It is exciting, but it lacks structure and substance. Hourly selling gives it the substance it needs so that you feel more like you have a real job.

You can decide how many hours your quota will be, and it certainly can be reviewed and changed from time to time. I use forty hours as a basis for comparison because that is the basic standard for full-time employment. You may want to work more or less, depending on your situation.

Within Domestic Counselors Inc., we keep a record of each person's hourly sales volume by dividing the total volume sold by the number of hours worked. If you do that for a few weeks, or preferably months, you will get a pretty accurate record for yourself. Multiply your commission rate by your hourly volume and you can do some pretty realistic income planning, because you know your number of hours will be constant.

Hourly selling makes the incalculable calculable. The sales field is full of ambiguities. If someone's sales are down, how can the problem be analyzed? Is it his attitude? Is it what he says on his appointments? Is it laziness? Is it the economy? There are so many variables! I was a math major in college, and when we were solving complex problems we looked for things that were constant. If one or two things are known, the unknown can be more easily discovered. When your effort (hourly commitment) is constant, you can analyze your sales more efficiently.

If your job involves a combination of selling and management, you must allow for that when setting your hours. Set them low enough to be realistic, but high enough to prevent you from using your management responsibilities as an excuse not to sell.

Whatever the case, hourly selling keeps you

working within a certain structure. It may seem like all of this structure will take some of the excitement out of selling. Well, it probably does, but the direction and peace of mind you will get will be worth it. Besides that, nothing is more exciting than increased sales!

6

The Mechanics of Hourly Selling

Once you are convinced that it makes good sense to establish a preset number of hours to spend on selling during each week, you immediately need a definition of what an hour of selling time is. This is probably the most controversial part of hourly selling, but I again urge you to keep an open mind as we proceed through this. I have heard some salespeople say that the only time they consider selling time is when they are actually putting on a call. To do that completely ignores all of the time you spent just to get you in front of that prospect. All of the activity you went through to obtain and organize your leads, all of the leads who were not home or would not look at your presentation, and all of the time it took you to drive to your appointment is ignored. If all of that time is not selling activity, I do not know what you would call it. If you are going to ignore or discount all of the time required to get you in front of your prospect, you might as well ignore all of the time you spend on a call except the actual signing of the order! That is the only time the customer is technically buying; therefore that is the only time you are technically selling. Signing a contract takes only about five seconds. So, using that logic, I only spend about fifty seconds a week selling!

We can get ridiculous with this example, but I think it is obvious that we must look at the entire scope of selling activity. I certainly agree that the actual signing of an order is the ultimate goal, and everything done during your selling time should be directed towards it. "Selling time", or "selling activity" if you prefer, should really be defined as all activities that are involved in obtaining, organizing, contacting, and giving a presentation to your prospect.

Hourly Selling takes the ultimate goal—a signed contract—and analyzes how you got there. It starts with the sale and follows the logic backwards. As you examine everything in reverse, you will discover that obtaining orders involves quite a variety of activities. These activities will vary somewhat from business to business, but the same principle applies.

Here is a list of activities that, in our business, I consider selling time:

1. Putting on a call
2. Contacting leads, either by phone or in person
3. Cold canvassing
4. Distributing mail-in cards
5. Searching for areas to sell in
6. Calling or stopping in on previous customers
7. Some driving time
8. Recopying and organizing leads
9. Filling out your weekly report.

FILLING OUT YOUR WEEKLY REPORT

I will elaborate on the last activity first because I can almost see the frowns as people read it. If your company does not require a weekly report, make an informal one just for your own use. You will need a place to keep a record of your hours anyway. I would be hard pressed to show how filling out your weekly report helps lead to a sale, except that part of the hourly system, by definition, requires you to keep a very accurate and honest record of your selling time. As a reward for going on the hourly system, and as an encouragement to get involved in it each day, I let filling out my weekly report count as selling time. I look at my selling as a neat package that is symbolized by what I put on my report. On Monday morning I start with a clean sheet with no hours or sales recorded on it. At the end of the week I always have exactly the number of hours on it that were my goal and, invariably, a number of sales as well. Each week's mounting sales confirm my theory yet again.

The essence and beauty of hourly selling is that whenever you start putting in time, you can pick and choose from any item considered as selling time. You can be as selfish and lazy as you wish as long as you stay within the rules and guidelines. It allows you to be as comfortable as possible at all times because you can choose the activity that you are in the mood for. It even allows you to slow your pace down to a minimum if that is how you feel at the moment, but it still forces you to continue on a path that will eventually lead to an order.

SALES CALLS

Let's go back to the first selling activity, putting on a call. Not much elaboration is needed for this one. Everybody pretty much agrees that this is selling time. You certainly need to put on calls to get sales. Closing percentages vary greatly, but the effort required to put on the call is very essential. Any time you spend in putting on a presentation to a prospect, regardless of whether or not they purchase anything, is definitely selling time.

CONTACTING LEADS

This next activity is selling time. If you are phoning or stopping in on your leads, you are making a very direct effort to have someone sit down and listen to your presentation. Without this activity you would never be in on a call and would never have the opportunity to get a signed order.

COLD CANVASSING

Cold canvassing is certainly selling time. In many direct-sales businesses it is one of the most frequently used ways to obtain leads. It is what separates direct sales from retail sales. We go to the customer rather than have the customer come to us. *Any activity that produces leads is selling time because it is supplying you with potential customers.*

MAIL-IN CARDS

Some businesses, including ours, have developed a mail-in card that can be distributed. As long as a mail-in card is proven to work, distributing it is selling time because, again, it is supplying you with leads. Our mail-in cards can be put on bulletin boards, under people's doors, and so on. Prospects who are potentially interested send them in, after which we contact them. If your business has a mail-in card, it is a nice addition to hourly selling.

SEARCHING FOR SELLING AREAS

If you decide to go cruising around searching for new areas to sell or cold canvass in, that is also selling time. It is an activity that eventually produces new prospects for you, which of course leads you one step closer to obtaining an appointment. Even if you spend time searching in an area which turns out not to be a good area, it can still be justified as selling time. Selling is an odds game: Give a certain number of demonstrations and you will get a certain number of sales; contact a certain number of prospects and you will get a certain number of appointments; do a given amount of prospecting and you will get a given number of prospects: check out a given number of areas and you will find the good areas to work in. If you discover that a certain area is not productive to work in, at least you will not waste any time on it again, which increases your chances of discovering a good area. Put in a given number of hours and you will, on the average, get a given amount of sales. Hourly selling is the ultimate way of recognizing that sales is an odds game.

CONTACTING PREVIOUS CUSTOMERS

Any time you use to call or stop in on a previous customer is definitely selling time. There are numerous and varied benefits of calling on people who have already bought from you. I check back on each of my customers after they receive their order. Whenever possible, I try to personally stop in rather than call them. This lets them know that I appreciate their business and am concerned about their order. This builds rapport with your clientele so they will have confidence to buy from you again someday. Sometimes when I check back I discover that they have a friend or roommate who is in the market for my products. Even sitting at your desk casually paging through your previous customer files can be considered selling time. Oftentimes you will be reminded of a customer to call on again for possible additional sales. The practice of calling your customers just to say hello lets them know that you have not forgotten them, and helps to maintain a good relationship with them that will pave the way for more sales. At worst, it is just good business to keep in contact with your customers.

Even if your reason for contacting a customer is a seemingly negative reason, it is still selling time. In the event they are unhappy with their order, the quicker you get the details and rectify the problem, the quicker good relations will be restored. Good customer service, which leads to good word-of-mouth advertising, results in additional future sales. Remember, hourly selling deals with averages over the long haul, not just with immediate results. Some of the results of your selling time may not become evident for months or even years, but that is all right. Hourly selling is directed more at the career person who is here to make a long-term business out of sales rather than just to make a fast buck on a temporary basis.

Another seemingly negative reason to call on a customer is if they have stopped making their payments. Your particular business will dictate to what extent the salesperson becomes involved in this. If you are contacting a customer for this reason, it is selling time. I put this into the category of *keeping the product sold*. In almost all sales, if an account stops paying, the salesperson is penalized to some degree. If we go back to the definition of hourly selling that says "enough business to pay you well for the time you spend," we will see the correlation. Every activity in the *hourly selling* plan, and especially this activity, is somehow directed at business that you will be paid for. One of the best examples of this would be insurance sales, where renewals are so important.

DRIVING TIME

It took me quite a while to reach a definition of when driving time should count as selling time. It cannot be so lenient that all day can be spent in the car, but it has to be flexible enough to be practical. To reach it, I observed a lot of *good* salespeople and also analyzed the downfalls of many failures who spent too much time in their cars. Realistically, most direct sales involves some driving time, so a certain amount has to be allowed. *Hourly Selling* has two driving-time rules.

The One-Hour Driving Rule

The first is that you may drive for up to one hour if you have an appointment with a prospect or a previous customer. I have seen many good salespeople drive for an hour to get to an appointment. If it is good enough for them, it is good enough for me. The time counts even if the appointment does not take place. The good intent on your part is what is important. Hourly selling rewards good work habits, regardless of whether or not they always pay off. Constant good work habits always pay off in the long run.

The Fifteen-Minute Driving Rule

The second driving rule is that if you are not on your way to an appointment, you can drive for no longer than fifteen minutes without stopping and checking an area for new leads, knocking on a door, putting out at least one mail-in card, or making a phone call to a prospect or customer. Again, the good intent on your part is all that is required. If you knocked on a door or made a call and there was no answer or the line was busy, it still counts. If every attempt every salesperson made paid off, we would all be millionaires in no time at all. Again hourly selling rewards consistent good efforts. I have seen many good salespeople cruise around for ten or fifteen minutes before getting into an area where they want to work. Theoretically, you could drive all day, stopping only once every fifteen minutes, and count all of it as selling time. Chances are, though, that if you have any selling instinct at all you will eventually get sick of this and finally settle on an area to work in for a while.

I use the fifteen-minute rule mostly when I am traveling from one area to another and want to make all my driving time count. My branch office is in St. Cloud, Minnesota, but our main office is in Minneapolis, which is about seventy miles away. Occasionally, if I am going to Minneapolis for a meeting or just to sell, I get selling time in on my way. There are small towns along the highway, none of which are more than fifteen minutes apart. I make a brief stop in each of them so that I can count my driving as selling time. As a result of this, I have developed sales in each of those towns during the past couple of years. A *good* salesperson probably checks out those towns for prospects while on his way through because he is more naturally motivated and has selling on his mind. The average salesperson of the second category I mentioned earlier almost never makes those stops. He just is not as naturally sales-conscious as a good salesperson. He has to wait until he is hyped up to sell. I am in that second category of average salespeople but I use hourly selling, and I make those stops just to fulfill its rules. It does not matter why I stop, the point is that I do. Hourly selling forces me to imitate a *good* salesperson's method. Any *average* salesperson who decides to use hourly selling will be able to imitate a *good* salesperson without altering his personality. Hourly selling allows for all the strengths and weaknesses of the salesperson. Since the time when I developed my formula for hourly selling, my sales totals have also imitated those of a *good* salesperson. The amazing thing is that my sales have risen, but my personality has not been altered and I have never had to get myself psyched up to go out and work. I just put together my formula for hourly selling and decided to believe that it really works and to follow its rules consistently.

One other benefit of the fifteen-minute rule is a physical one. It forces you to get out of your car and move around at least that often. You stay physically, and therefore mentally, fresher if you do not sit in your car for too long at any one time.

Even though stopping in an unlikely place just to fulfill the minimum requirement may sometimes seem a little ridiculous, it will result in occasional sales in some unlikely places. It might make you appear "lucky" to other salespeople. Remember earlier when I described the *good* salesperson as seeming "luckier" than the rest of us? By making these little "hunch" stops, you imitate a *good* salesperson once again.

ORGANIZING YOUR LEADS

Time spent organizing and recopying your leads on cards or in whatever kind of bookkeeping system you have is also selling time. If you go through a list of leads on a paper, crossing them out as you contact them, you end up with a pretty messy piece of paper. Any good leads remaining on a piece of scribbled-up paper never look as positive as they would if they were freshly recopied. It will also help you to forget occasional negative experiences you may have had with those old, crossed-out names. Most people agree that it is smart to organize your leads geographically before going out selling. Spending a few minutes putting your leads in the order in which you are going to hit them will make you more efficient. My leads are always neatly copied and organized. They always look positive. I will usually do my organizing while sipping coffee in a restaurant. That is pretty low-key selling time, but it is an essential part of getting some organizing done and is helping to get me involved. As I look through my leads, I invariably start to feel like going out and talking to them. It gets my motors turning, especially on Monday morning. A salesperson who was number one in the nation for his company once told me that each day he made a list of his leads in the geographical order in which he was going to drive to them. It made him feel more official, like all he had to do was make his rounds like a delivery person. The job of selling is as official as you want to make it. When a salesperson is having trouble and his spirits are low, he is suffering from a low self-image. He barely feels like he has a job. It is at times like that when a salesperson is tempted to quit sales and get a normal job with some substance and regularity. Hourly selling helps provide that substance and regularity. You are literally punching a clock: Fortunately, however, it is still your own.

BREAKS

You can take up to fifteen minutes for a break, sometimes as often as every two hours, and still count it as selling time. The reasoning behind this rule was obtained from observing two sources. The first source is from those people with "normal" jobs. Whether it is factory or office work, many people get morning and afternoon coffee breaks of ten or fifteen minutes in length, and they are usually paid for them. The morning breaks are customarily scheduled approximately two hours after starting time and two hours before the noon lunch hour. If someone starts work at 8:00 A.M., his morning break is probably scheduled for around 10:00 A.M. The afternoon breaks are similarly scheduled so that they provide a break after about two hours of work.

Short breaks help worker morale and alertness. In some cases, as in factory or construction work, they also probably contribute to worker safety.

I figure that a salesperson deserves a refreshing break as much as a person with a "normal" job. Notice how I refer to jobs other than sales as being "normal," the implication being that sales is an "abnormal" profession. In many ways sales *is* abnormal. It is most abnormal in the sense of time structure. In almost all of our experience in school or other jobs, we are conditioned to accept having our time disciplined for us. By the time a person graduates from high school, he has had twelve years of conditioning that essentially says: Be at school during certain hours or you are in trouble. If you go on to college, the schedule becomes a little more flexible because you can choose which classes to take, but once one is chosen, it is still held at a specified time, and if you are not there, you miss out.

Beyond the strong influence of school during our growing-up years is our cumulative work experience. In almost all jobs, except for sales, you must be at work during a certain time period. If you do not show up, you will be fired.

Whether it is school or work experience, most of us have never been taught that time discipline is our responsibility. You can see, then, how sales is so unconventional. A person who enters sales suddenly has a responsibility in the area of time discipline that he has had no conditioning for. Worst of all, his survival in sales depends on it. It is not that I feel that humans are incapable of learning that discipline, it is just that most of us have never had to. Humans are very adaptable, but adaptations are rarely made until the need for them arises. Starting a sales career is challenging enough for most people. They have to learn their particular business, how to deal with people, and how to handle rejection. Those are the apparent obstacles, but the silent killer is time discipline.

I have seen some of the finest, sharpest people come into sales and fall flat on their faces. They are very personable with people and quickly learn to give a persuasive sales call. They have been leaders in their communities or presidents of business clubs in their schools and would be recommended by many as "most likely to succeed in sales." I am sorry to say that their failure rates are the same as anyone else's. They have the same deficiency in regard to time discipline as everyone else.

I feel that more people could succeed in sales if they had more knowledge and experience in disciplining their time. The problem is that, with all of the other challenges that a sales job involves, most salespeople quit the business before they get a chance to realize that time discipline is their real problem. I can think of very few ways that a salesperson can gain experience with or knowledge of time discipline.

This book is the first official sales-improvement manual that deals exclusively with time discipline. The information here will make you more knowledgeable on the subject while offering a specific plan to conquer it.

Everything in the hourly selling plan is directed at making you feel like you have a "normal" job. The more you feel like you have a "normal" job, the more you can draw on resources you have developed from your past schooling or job experience. Every profession has its "clock watchers." Their goal is just to work until the next coffee break, or until the lunch hour or quitting time. With hourly selling you can actually get away with being a "clock watcher" during your selling time. "Only twenty minutes more until I can take a break; I think I can work that much longer," or "only an hour to quitting time," can be the thoughts that keep you going, rather than another pep talk about "getting those sales."

The other source of the rule on taking breaks has come from observing good salespeople. I have seen many of them take short breaks while out selling. The important thing is that they keep their breaks short and get right back to selling. The rest of us from the second category will do the same thing, but we will be doing it to fulfill the requirements of hourly selling. We need more specific guidelines or our breaks may last forty-five minutes or longer. We just are not as naturally motivated to control our break time. We need specific guidelines. How long can a break be? Answer: Fifteen minutes. How often? Answer: No more often than every two hours.

Don't misunderstand. You can take longer breaks, but you just can't count the extra time as selling time. Let's say you take a break that ends up lasting forty-five minutes because you get involved in reading the newspaper. That is fine, but you cannot count the last half hour of your break as selling time because, technically, you quit selling after the deserved first fifteen minutes were used up.

As you become accustomed to using hourly selling, you will probably seldom take more than the usual fifteen minutes because you realize that that time will have to be made up for later in the week. I am not saying that you will always use every break you deserve. If you get involved in selling and putting on calls, you may go for much longer without a break. The rule on breaks is to get you through the tough times.

Actually, hourly selling is designed to get you through the tough times. I can document scores of times that I have gotten sales while being a "clock watcher." When I go out selling, I usually have a certain number of hours that I plan to spend selling on that particular day. I keep each day's totals to be sure that my weekly quota will be fulfilled by the end of the week. By having a certain number of hours in mind, I am automatically establishing "quitting time" for the day. If things are not going well and I am not very motivated, I keep punching the clock because a "break" or "quitting time" is just a few minutes away. What happens sometimes is that during those few extra minutes I run into a good prospect and make a sale. In that case, I exceed my intended number of hours for the day, but I also have that much less time to work the rest of the week. Entire sales meetings can be given on "putting out that extra effort" and how you often get sales by pushing yourself to stay motivated a little longer. Being a "clock watcher" while using hourly selling produces the same result without the need to stay "motivated" in some mysterious way.

There are also the obvious reasons to build breaks into selling time. It is just plain refreshing. You feel much more like working if you stop to catch your breath once in a while.

The central rule of hourly selling is that to have

your time count as "selling time" you must constantly be doing one of the previously listed selling activities. You can be ambitiously cold canvassing or casually paging through your leads, but it all counts as long as you are doing something. Breaks must be allowed for, but some realistic guidelines must be established.

If it bothers you to include things like calling delinquent accounts or organizing your leads in your weekly requirement of hours, just add a few hours to your requirement to allow for those activities. That way everything is kept in a neat, controllable package of time each week. The only unpredictables in your work week are meetings, general office work, and managing, if you are involved in any management. It will help you maintain a clear-cut definition of when you are selling and when you are doing office work. All of your selling activity with your own customers is included in your selling hours, but any other office or management work is not.

7

Implementing the Mechanics

The rules of hourly selling may seem rather tedious, but applying them is actually fairly easy. The timekeeping, which is probably the most aggravating part, can be kept fairly simple. Once you start your selling time, all your normal activities will probably easily qualify as selling time. Just keep in mind the fifteen-minute rule for driving time. Once you are out working, all of the time counts, even if you only use your car to go down the street a few blocks. The only thing the driving rule says is that if you are going to do some driving you cannot drive for more than fifteen minutes without stopping and making at least a brief selling effort. Otherwise, none of that driving time counts. In most cases, if your day is spent in the same town or general area, you probably will not have to worry about the fifteen-minute rule.

Let's step through a couple of sample selling days as an example. Assume it is 1:00 P.M. and you are at the office. You have already attended a sales meeting and taken care of any miscellaneous office work. There are still a few salespeople milling around the office after the sales meeting, and you are tempted to sit around and socialize with them. However, you have committed yourself to hourly selling, and you therefore decide to start putting in some time. You write down 1:00 P.M. on your note pad and pick up your pack of leads. Make one phone call to a lead so your driving time will count when you leave the office. If there is no answer, it does not matter, you are now officially selling. After you hang up the phone, you go out the door and get into your car. You have no appointments and are not even sure where you are going. After you drive a few blocks and are out of sight of the office, you pull over and stop. Now you are free from distractions and can go through your leads or decide where to start prospecting. Now you can relax and start to sell. That's right, relax and start to sell! You have isolated yourself. You cannot get a phone call, a piece of mail, or anything else that could frustrate your selling intentions. All the numerous potential distractions have been left behind. Relax and work at your own pace. The pace that salespeople are comfortable with varies greatly, so you now proceed at whatever pace is most comfortable for you.

While looking through your leads, you find one who works nights and might be home during the day. It is about a twenty-five-minute drive away, so you start in that direction, but you watch for a place to make one stop along the way so you will not violate the fifteen-minute rule. After about ten minutes you notice an apartment building, so you stop and do some cold canvassing. Out of eight doors that you hit in that building, only one person is home, but you make an appointment for a demonstration at 11:00 A.M. the next day. You now proceed to the original lead, only to discover that no one is home. The remainder of the afternoon is spent cold canvassing and talking to a few people that you manage to catch at home. You have discovered a good area to work in, which may result in a number of good sales over the next two weeks. You also stop at the cleaners and pick up a suit that you left there a few days ago. You are in the cleaners for ten minutes and must therefore deduct that time. To keep the time recording simple, just keep moving up your starting time. So you change the starting time on your note pad from 1:00 P.M. to 1:10 P.M. and continue working.

At 4:10 you stop at home and have dinner. You finish eating and are back out selling by 5:00. You must deduct those fifty minutes. Move your starting time up to 2:00 P.M. By 6:00 P.M. you are in on a demonstration which results in a sale. You are out of that appintment by 7:30 P.M. Your throat is dry, so you stop for ten to fifteen minutes to have a coke.

No need to deduct that time. Even factories give their workers brief coffee breaks in the morning and afternoon.

You spend the remainder of the evening lining up appointments for each of the next two evenings and checking on a customer delivery. By 9:00 P.M. you arrive home and make a quick call to a lead so the final driving time to get home can be counted. The starting time on your pad is 2:00 P.M. and the quitting time is 9:00 P.M. Enter seven hours of selling time for that day on your weekly report.

Only seven hours, huh? That morning you had to leave home at 9:00 A.M. to get to the sales meeting on time. 9:00 A.M. to 9:00 P.M. is twelve hours. Without hourly selling it would be easy to say that you put in a twelve-hour day. You may have been *at work* for twelve hours, but you have *worked* or *sold* for only seven hours. Only seven productive hours! Hourly selling shocks you into being honest about your productivity. How many of us have wished there were more hours in a day? If we cannot manufacture more hours, the least we can do is keep better track of what happens during the hours we do have.

Morning of the second day comes. No sales meeting today. Maybe you have an early golf game or racquetball match, or you just spend some time at home. Whatever the case, you start your selling time at 10:30 A.M. when you leave for your 11:00 A.M. appointment. Since you are on the way to an appointment, there is no need to follow the fifteen-minute rule. Remember, up to one hour of nonstop driving time is allowed if you are going to a call.

After making the sale on that call, you arrive at the office at 12:45 P.M. You spend the next two hours doing some paperwork and going out to lunch with a couple of other salespeople from the office. To deduct those two hours, you move the starting time on your note pad up to 12:30 P.M. After that you sell straight through, giving two calls, neither of which is successful, and arrive home at 9:30 P.M. Let's see—today's starting time was 12:30 and quitting time was 9:30—your hours today totaled nine. That is not bad! You had a little time off in the morning, and you also stopped to socialize at the office for a while. A fairly enjoyable day! In addition to that, you have the satisfaction of knowing that you put out a good work effort.

Schedules vary greatly. If you have some administrative or management responsibilities, maybe you can break away to sell for only an hour or two during the daytime. Those few hours will, on the average, help to narrow your work down to those hours of the evening when many prospects are at home. Whatever the case, set your hourly requirement low enough so that it allows you to get your office work done, but high enough so that it forces you to leave the office when the essentials are done. Once you rationally determine a number of hours for yourself, you must *never* deviate from it. You may periodically review how your hours suit your business and leisure goals and make occasional changes. However, I caution against making changes more often than every few months.

On Monday morning I know that absolutely nothing and nobody will come between me and my hours during that week. We all have unexpected things that come up in our business or personal lives and threaten to consume our time. If I get a lot of distractions during a given week, I become very unsociable as the weekend draws near. I start to avoid anything that may prevent me from getting my hours in.

If you have a job where you punch a clock for a company, you will get your hours in with them regardless of what happens. If some friends or relatives were to visit you unexpectedly, they would not be offended if you had to go to work at a job with regular hours. If you are in sales, however, many people will say, "You are your own boss, so you can take a day or two off if you want to." They are partially right, because you probably will not be fired for skipping a couple of days as you would be if you were working for someone else. What is happening, though, is that you are slowly firing yourself, because without consistent sales you may go broke. The saddest thing about that is that when a salesperson fails because of that lack of discipline, he usually blames the business instead of himself. Hourly selling forces you to constantly watch yourself and lets you know that if you fail, it will not be because of lack of effort.

One saleswoman in my group who very successfully used hourly selling was at first quite shocked to find out how hard it was to get her predetermined hours in. I explained to her that it does not just happen. Write down a rough estimate at the beginning of each week of how many hours you plan to get in each day, and make the final day the catch-all day for any remaining hours.

Probably the hardest thing for me to do has been to walk away from paperwork that needs to be done. I have always prided myself on being organized and having my desk in order. After all, a good businessman is well organized, right? Wrong! Not if the paperwork takes priority over profit. If my primary source of profit is making sales, then everything else can go to hell until I get my selling hours in. If there are not any sales, there will not be any paperwork anyway.

Office work or socializing at the office can very easily become a subconscious excuse for not going out selling. The fallacy that many salespeople operate under is that if they are "at the office" they are then "at work." If they are "at work," they tell themselves they are working. They are "at work," but they are doing little or nothing to obtain a sale, which is the actual purpose of their job.

The chain of events can happen something like this: A salesperson (let's call him Joe) attends a sales meeting at 10:00 A.M. It is a super meeting. It starts with some company cheers that are fun and silly but generate lots of enthusiasm. There is an excellent talk on keeping a positive attitude while selling. Many new ideas and sales techniques are discussed. After the meeting everyone decides to go out to lunch together. It is a fun lunch. Everyone is joking and talking about past sales. "Gosh," says Joe to himself, "it feels so good to be with all of these successful, positive people!" By the time everyone gets back from lunch it is 1:00 P.M. Some sales-people, especially the *good* ones, leave to go out selling. However, Joe remains at the office. There are still a few people hanging around socializing. Joe thinks of going out selling, but the picture of himself out there alone, searching for a prospect, seems far removed from all of this positiveness. He hangs around, visiting, until everyone else has left. It is now 3:00 P.M. and he sits down at his desk and does about an hour of paperwork. He is just start-ing to feel a little uneasy and says to himself, "I'd better get out selling," when a couple of the sales-people who left at 1:00 P.M. return to the office all excited about sales they just got. They ask Joe to go with them to get a sandwich. Quite relieved, Joe quickly accepts.

It is 5:00 P.M. when they return laughing and joking. Joe is positive and excited again, just like after the meeting that morning. The other sales-people leave and Joe is alone again, sitting at his desk. He feels a sudden feeling of fear but brushes it off by doing a half hour of paperwork and organiz-ing. He finally picks up his leads and guiltily makes one or two calls. One lead is not home and the other one is very negative. Joe is now feeling frustrated. Why can't he have a stack of leads like the other salespeople? He feels frustrated with himself and wishes he had gone out selling sooner. He even feels sleepy now. It seems too late in the evening to go out and find a good sale. The next and final emotion Joe feels—depression—is now starting to overtake him. But Joe is not a quitter. In a very withdrawn mood, he forces himself to go out cold canvassing. Joe thinks of a television show that he would really like to see. It is on in an hour...

Ever see some of yourself in Joe? Throughout this book I will try to make a strong case for hourly selling. The idea of hourly selling is fairly easy to understand, and the details are rather elementary. My real purpose in this book is to really convince you to go on an hourly selling system. However, you must first be totally convinced that all the inconveniences and details of hourly selling are worth the benefit.

It is a "one-system-covers-all" system. I could dig through company meeting files or my notes from numerous motivational speakers I have heard and give you example upon example of good work habits. Things such as "starting early" or "putting out that extra effort" make good meeting topics. It is easy to tell people to be positive, but when do you hear about practical ways to stay positive? It is impossible to feel positive all of the time. With hourly selling, however, it does not matter. You simply pick something to do that is more low-key but still considered selling time. Hourly selling is a way of pretending that you never become negative. With hourly selling it is nice to never have to wonder if you are following good selling habits. Otherwise, there are so many good selling habits to remember. Work hard, work long hours, don't stay in your car for too long, take care of your customers, do some cold canvassing, search for new areas to sell in, keep your leads organized, be persistent, don't take too many or too-long breaks, get out selling rather than socializing too much at the office...the list goes on and on and you have probably heard them all anyway. The hourly selling plan takes care of all of that in one simple package. Just complete your hours each week and stay within the rules, and you will automatically follow all of those *good* selling habits!

If you use a little creativity in applying the guidelines, you can come up with some unusual, if not amusing, results. Hourly selling makes an attempt to simulate a "normal" job while retaining as much freedom and flexibility as possible. In many regular jobs the worker knows how many hours he will be required to work, and while he is at work he fills that time with the activities of his assigned job. A direct-sales job can be approached in the same way.

By setting your hours, you know exactly how much time you will be working, and with an established list of selling activities as covered in Chapter 6, you know what your assigned selling job includes.

You will have the flexibility to put your hours in when and where you wish. You can vary your pace and switch from one selling activity to another anytime you want. Even if you decide to work at one of your least favorite activities for a while, it can be made more bearable by the knowledge that you can switch to another one whenever you really want to. Furthermore, you receive the satisfaction of knowing that you have put some more time in.

The guidelines can be stretched to cater to your needs, but at the same time they practically trick you into getting sales. Since your only goal is to get your hours in each week, you can devise ways to get extra time in here and there. Remember, once your time is in for the week, you *must* quit and have some time off. That can be a real incentive to work! You may find yourself starting much earlier in the day just to get some extra time in. You are inadvertently developing the *good* selling habit of starting early.

One of the rules most fun to toy with is the fifteen-minute driving rule. Hardly any of my driving time throughout the day is wasted. Remember, in order to count the driving time between two points, all that you have to do is attempt a phone call or knock on at least one door at each point. If I am at home and am leaving to go play racquetball, I make one call at home, and when I get to the club I pick up a phone and try calling another lead. It is about a fifteen-minute drive to get there, so I pick up an easy fifteen minutes of selling time. If that is done four times a week, I get in a whole hour towards my quota. The same thing can be done in driving from home to the office. In case a place I am driving to is further than a fifteen-minute drive away, I must make a stop somewhere along the way to keep from spending more than fifteen minutes in the car. When I stop I may check a house or an apartment building for new leads, drop off a mail-in card somewhere, or even look for a phone booth to make a call from. The result is that all of the driving time can be counted. I do the same thing while running errands during the day. If I am at the office and have to drive to a shopping center to get something, I make one phone call at the office and another call from a pay phone when I get to the shopping center, or I look for a place to do some brief cold canvassing in that area. Whatever actual time I spend in the store cannot be counted because while shopping I have ceased any kind of qualified selling activity. As soon as I walk out, however, my selling time starts again, and I become conscious of making selling stops or phone calls. Likewise, if I stop to fill the car with gas, I deduct the time I spend at the gas station, but my selling time immediately resumes when I leave.

You do not have to work selling time in like that, but it is a way to fulfill your weekly quota sooner. Once you realize how demanding your quota of hours is, you will look desperately for little tricks to use for getting extra time in. It may sound absurd, but it works. It may appear that you are working in a minimal amount of selling time around your errands, but you are actually working errands in around constant sales consciousness, which is a trait of a *good* salesperson. An *average* salesperson of the second category would seldom be that sales-conscious while running errands.

The *average* salesperson usually waits until all of his errands are done before he starts selling. He feels that he has to "get set" mentally before he can sell. Consequently, his errands probably take longer because nothing compels him to get right back to work. An *average* salesperson using hourly selling conquers that problem because he steadily racks up easy selling time. What is actually happening, though, is that he is keeping his mind on selling activities and talking to people. It may be sporadic, but it is better than nothing at all, and when he is done running errands, his motors will already be turning so he will be more prepared to settle into some constant selling time.

In addition to that psychological benefit, there is the fact that some actual productive results will occur. I can think of many sales I made as a result of just "putting my time in." When I am really lazy or negative, I call one of those leads that are "never home." Remember, a call attempt is all that is necessary. If the line is busy or no one is home, it still counts. When I am making sporadic calls throughout the day so that I can count my driving time between areas, I sometimes keep calling one of those "never-home" leads. Guess what eventually happens? I end up getting an answer, in which case I either burn out the lead or end up with a sale. In either event, my mission with that lead is finally over. Remember, my only reason for continuously calling a lead like that was to fulfill a requirement of hourly selling. I did not need to be super-motivated, because I was just getting some easy selling time in. Let's look again at what was actually happening. I had to be very persistent to finally catch that person at home. Maybe they had a busy or unusual schedule. What better way to catch them than to keep trying at all hours of the day? Hourly selling tricked me into the *good* selling habit of being persistent.

I should pause here to emphasize that I do not always work the hourly selling guidelines to that kind of minimum. I do work in blocks of pure selling time that consist of several hours of putting on calls and contacting leads. When possible, however, I prefer working a few hours at a time. The hours really breeze by when all is going well and sales are being made. Hourly selling is for good as well as the bad times.

The guidelines and philosophies of Hourly selling are something that can help to pull you through the bad times. Whether you are getting some easy time in by using the fifteen-minute driving rule or just working until your next break or your quitting time, you have very specific attainable little goals to attain, and if all of these little goals are attained, a larger goal of increased sales will also be realized.

A blend of selling activities will give the most variety and enjoyment to a selling day. I almost always start the day with a phone call to a lead before I leave home so that the time it takes me to drive to wherever I am going will count. I may make several calls, but at least one is required. Because I do this, I catch many leads that are home early in the day, which often leads to early-morning appointments. After I leave home, I may go cold-canvassing for an hour or so. This produces leads and sometimes an immediate sale. At worst, I discover the good and the bad areas to work in. If I have to make any miscellaneous stops, such as to put gas in the car or to run personal errands, I get those done, keeping the driving rule in mind and deducting from my selling time any actual time I spend on those interruptions. After that I may stop at a restaurant for coffee. If I bring my leads in to organize or recopy them, all of that can be counted as selling time. However, sitting there daydreaming or reading the newspaper cannot be counted. I can switch to a low-key activity like organizing leads, but I must constantly be doing something that qualifies as selling time. If I stop for lunch, the time I spend eating cannot be counted. That is a lunch break, not a coffee break.

I also make routine stops at my office. Depending on what needs doing, I will spend anywhere from fifteen minutes to a few hours at the office on any given day. Any general office work is *not* selling time. I can count selling time at the office only if I am talking to prospects on the phone or in person or organizing leads, and so on. If a friend or fellow salesperson stops in and visits for a half hour, that interruption must be deducted from my selling time. The important thing is: When time-consuming things such as opening mail or socializing at the office are over, you must get right back to selling, not necessarily because you are that motivated but because you have made a commitment to spend a given amount of hours on selling.

Hourly selling forces you to record how time-consuming general ofice work and socializing can be. One time I stopped by the office with the intent of quickly opening my mail and doing some paperwork that could not wait any longer. I sped through it because I wanted to get back to my selling time. It ended up taking an entire hour, which wasn't bad, but if I had estimated how long I was there I would probably have said about half an hour. When you are busy, time can go faster than you think. Hourly selling allows absolutely no estimates. Never say that a break was "about an hour" or "I worked about three hours." If you are laughing and joking with other people around the office, an hour can seem like twenty minutes.

Remember, if you are paid on the basis of your sales volume, any time at the office other than qualified selling time is nonproductive. Hourly selling forces you to get the nonproductive necessities done and return to selling. Hourly selling does not forbid you from socializing at the office, but it requires you to keep track of the time you spend doing it, and to deduct that time from your selling time. When you can clearly see how it affects your productive time, you may decide that it is not always worth it. Every nonproductive hour I spend at the office means one less hour for leisure or family time to me, because I know I have to fulfill my quota of selling time.

By deciding to "set your hours" on an hourly system you have, in effect, decided to become successful. Come hell or high water, you are going to get your time in each week. Those productive hours, flexible as they are, are your number-one priority. A person with a "normal" job has the same priority, but he doesn't have to think about it so much. He accepts the fact that his employer has hired him to work for a certain number of hours per week. But if you are a salesperson, you *do* have to think about it. You are the one controlling your destiny.

One selling activity that I do at my office is to page through my customer files and randomly call previous customers to see if they want to buy more or just to say hello. That results in sales and better customer relations. Since it qualifies as selling time, I get some more fairly easy and enjoyable time in. What is actually happening is that I am taking good care of my customers, which is, again, a trait of a *good* salesperson. You also receive some indirect motivation when talking to your customers because they help to remind you of your past successes.

Whether it is calling previous customers, organizing leads, cold canvassing, dropping in on prospects, or making phone calls there are a variety of activities and variations to choose from. These options make it easier to choose an activity that you are in the mood for at the time. The amazing thing is that it does not seem to matter in what order they are done, as long as they all get done over the long haul. A salesperson's mood will vary from very positive and ambitious to quite negative and withdrawn. The activities can be chosen and manipulated in forms that can fit almost any mood.

Just keeping active can improve a low mood, and stumbling across a good sale can really get you going. Let's say you are feeling lazy and are just plugging along to get your time in. All you need is one positive prospect, and your entire mood snaps to life. Hourly selling keeps you out working until those things happen.

Positive motivational slogans and hyped-up sales meetings do little to get me excited anymore. People buying my products is what gets me excited! Hourly selling keeps me working until that happens. When I have a big week in sales, people often say that I must have really been excited to accomplish that. Yes, the sales made me excited, but excitement is not what got me started. My commitment to hourly selling got me out working and the resulting sales made me excited. Hourly selling is a natural high!

Hourly selling does not always prove itself right away. When I make a sale, I always try to remember back to where the lead originated from. Sometimes it came from my efforts of several weeks ago, or at a time when I was working at a low-key pace. Hourly selling does not guarantee everything in the short run, but in the long run it provides solid average consistency. It deals with long-term averages which are very powerful. Naturally, not every effort pays off, but when you do hit on the good sales, your average is brought up.

There come times when a salesperson feels so unmotivated or out of leads that it seems impossible to get more sales. When that happens to me, I give up. I mentally quit. I say to myself, "I am now so totally convinced that I cannot get any more sales that I'm not even going to hope for sales: I am now truly going to be on an hourly system because the only thing that I feel I can do is to put my time in. I am going to put my time in so I can say that I put out the effort, but I know I will not get any sales." On that premise, I start putting my hours in with no expectation of a sale. The pressure to sell is now off because I have given up. The only reason I keep working is that I plan to fulfill my predetermined quota of hours. That way, if I fail, I will know it will not be because I didn't put out an effort.

After this whole process, I take a second look at what is about to happen. I think forward a few weeks. If, for example, my present weekly quota is forty hours, I will be working a total of 160 hours over the next four weeks. Since I know those hours will be worked, it starts to seem unlikely that I won't get at least a few sales during that time. The result is that I invariably get sales; I often get many more than I ever dreamed of when I was so negative. The results don't always come when you want them, but they do eventually come. Hourly selling is not a "quick fix"; it is a "permanent fix."

The part of hourly selling that is hardest to adjust to is probably the actual timekeeping. Writing down starting and stopping times and recording your breaks can be tedious. Furthermore, you must keep track of your time down to the minute. *No estimates are allowed.* Saying that you worked for "about ten minutes" or "about an hour" is unacceptable. It can be easy to overestimate, so to avoid that, keep track of every minute each day. It is also more satisfying to know that you did not cheat on your time *at all.*

8

*Calculating
Time Off*

If you plan to hold yourself strictly to your hourly quota each week, you need a way to realistically calculate justifiable time off. These guidelines are a combination of what would probably be allowed if you had a regular job and what a *good* salesperson would do.

ALLOWABLE INTERRUPTIONS

The first justifiable time off is in the category of *allowable interruptions,* or small breaks that need not be deducted from your selling time. You may certainly take a ten- or fifteen-minute break every two or three hours without deducting those minutes. Morning and afternoon coffee breaks are allowed on most jobs. Even *good* salespeople take an occasional break to refresh themselves. Other similar interruptions can be handled the same way. Say you are out working and you run across a friend who invites you to stop and visit for a few minutes. The first fifteen minutes need not be deducted. The important thing is to keep the break short and to resume selling. Let's say your visit lasted longer than fifteen minutes. If, for example, it lasted a half hour, you need to deduct only fifteen minutes from your selling time because the first fifteen minutes was an allowable break. The intention here is to allow some normal flexibility, but also to keep some limits on minor breaks.

ALLOWABLE DEDUCTIONS

The other justifiable time off can be referred to as *allowable deductions*. They are circumstances for which you can honestly deduct a certain amount of hours from your usual quota for a given week. Before we go further, we need a definition of what a *day* is. A day's worth of hours is simply one fifth of your weekly quota. I use "one fifth" simply because we are comparing your hours with those of a regular job, which is usually based on a five-day work week. If your quota is forty hours, then one working day is eight hours. If you take two days off for some allowable reason, you deduct two days' worth of hours from your quota for that week. You may, of course, put those remaining hours in on any days of that week that you wish.

Vacation Time

If hourly selling is to be used to make your job seem more like other jobs, some vacation time needs to be allowed. Your conscience, along with an idea of how much time some other jobs allow, should help you to decide how much vacation time you can take each year. Many people get at least one week of vacation time per year. If they stay with their companies for a number of years, their vacation time is customarily increased to two, three, or even four weeks. Remember, one week is defined as whatever your weekly quota is. You could look at it as your total "vacation hours" each year. Those vacation hours can be declared on any week you wish, either a few at a time or all at once. Again, the choices are all yours. The key is to determine them ahead of time.

Holidays

You can take any major holiday off. Again, one day off, for example Labor Day, is one fifth of your weekly quota. By being honest with yourself, you can determine which ones to justify as off time. If you need a definition of a holiday, use days that are legal holidays.

Sometimes you can take a few vacation hours, combine them with a holiday, and end up with a four-day weekend.

Sick Leave

If you wake up in the morning and are too sick to work (this also requires you to be honest with yourself), deduct one day's worth of hours from that week's quota. Do this each day until you are well enough to work. Sick leave has to be allowed for. You could go crazy trying to make up for several sick days in a week.

Conventions

Any major company convention or major group training session can allow you those days off. Even *good* salespeople attend conventions. For example, if you are leaving for a convention on Thursday morning, you can subtract two days from your quota, because that Thursday and Friday will be spent at the convention. Routine weekly meetings, however, cannot be deducted. Things like that should be taken into consideration when you set your weekly quota.

Unforeseen Emergencies

You must be careful what you allow in this category, but be realistic: There are some things that come up which affect you but are totally beyond your control.

One evening a tornado ripped through our city while I was out selling. When I heard the warnings, I stopped selling and headed home. I had originally planned on putting in two more hours that day, so I just deducted two hours from that week's quota. However, be careful not to use a minor rainstorm to justify time off.

If you have a funeral to attend, or a serious family emergency comes up, common sense would say that time can be taken off.

It is necessary to be honest with yourself on these matters. One way of deciding is to ask yourself, "Would I take time off for this emergency if I had a regular job?"

The beauty of all these calculations is that they put an end to ambiguous excuses, such as "I had a slow week because I was sick" or "It was Christmas time," and so on.

9

*Prevent
Job Burnout*

Hourly selling also has a psychological effect: Once a salesperson has adapted to the hourly selling attitude, many selling situations that commonly cause stress are no longer stressful. That "an-hour-of-work-is-an-hour-of-work" kind of attitude is sort of relaxing. Once you are convinced that all you have to do is follow the rules of hourly selling and everything will eventually work out, you are freed from a lot of pressure. The pressure to hurry up and get a sale is removed. Just put your time in and the sales will come.

Many salespeople are quite competitive; however, some not only try to outsell other salespeople, but they also view each and every appointment they have as a win-or-lose situation. They win if they make the sale and lose if they do not. Even when making a door approach, it is win or lose. Every time they are up against a prospect, their talents and egos are on the line. That might be fun and challenging for a while, but it is much healthier to develop a more stable attitude toward a career.

Door approaches and sales calls are all in a day's work for me. Naturally, I always hope for a sale, but I am basically content just to get my hours in. Most salespeople become quite frustrated if they are delayed in traffic or have to wait for a train. I am not pleased by those situations either, but since it is a situation beyond my control, I am still getting my time in. I also believe that this attitude makes you much calmer when you do get in front of a prospect.

I always feel like I have accomplished something at the end of each day. You feel a kind of self-respect when you know that you have put out an effort, even if you did not get a sale that particular day.

Sometimes when someone asks me how I did, I have to stop and think. I feel so good about my day that I forget that I have not actually sold anything. Of course, many times I do have sales to report. But even if I have not sold anything, you can bet that I have probably dug up some good leads or lined up some appointments. At worst, I have probably gotten rid of some bad leads that I would have had to spend time on later. How much healthier of an attitude can there be? To actually feel good about not making a sale. I am either very stable or very psychotic!

Hourly selling concentrates more on the general mental comfort of the salesperson rather than ramming a bunch of PMA slogans down his throat. If a salesperson is always comfortable when he is out working, he will find it easier to discipline himself to stay out working.

While out selling, a salesperson goes through a lot of feelings. On the positive side are excitement, acceptance, warmth, enthusiasm, exhilaration, confidence, and sometimes even overconfidence. On the negative side are rejection, depression, guilt, inadequacy, failure, bitterness, and anticipation of more failure. Hourly selling eliminates or, at least, reduces the negative feelings, and it retains but tones down the positive ones; it guards against overconfidence, that problem of feeling that you are so good that too much time off is justified. At any rate, the extreme highs and lows are somewhat evened out. Admittedly, some of the excitement is taken away, but the added peace of mind is worth it.

Since I have been saying that many of the conventional attitudes towards motivation should be thrown out, you may be asking what I replace them with. First of all, I prefer to look at it, like Zig Ziglar says, as "enjoying the price" rather than "paying the price" of success. Since hourly selling allows me to choose from many different selling activities, I can selfishly pick whatever I am in the mood for. I allow myself to be as comfortable as possible at all times. When I "punch in" and start my selling time for the day is when I start thinking about what I feel like doing. If a salesperson has been talking to customers all day and has made a few sales, it is easy for him to be enthusiastic. But how about those first couple of door approaches of the day, especially if after a weekend or vacation? You have not had business on your mind for a few days and are just not into being happy and enthusiastic with people. How do you get your motors turning? Well, you don't have to get your motors turning, at least not very fast to begin with. You can start slowly with something that is not too demanding, such as checking for new names in apartments, putting out mail-in cards, or maybe confirming some deliveries of previous sales. Maybe you can just sit and go through your leads for a few minutes. Just *try* to reorganize your leads without getting a little bit more positive. You are bound to see a good lead that you dug up a while ago. Even neatly recopying your old leads on a fresh piece of paper will make them look more inviting. One reason that knocking on doors has become easier for me is that my leads always look so neat and organized that I can't wait to discover which one will be a buyer. I agree that sitting and recopying leads as such does not directly lead you to a sale. However, can you see how it is indirectly motivating you to feel good about going out selling? Hourly selling does not pretend to be totally efficient, but it is wholesomely motivating. And consistent motivation is one of our real goals.

I suppose being totally efficient could be defined as constantly knocking on doors and giving demonstrations from morning to night. But let's be honest about it; how many people can get motivated and stay motivated to do that constantly week after week, year after year? Probably only a few of those superproducers. But remember, hourly selling is not meant for those salespeople anyway. I have seen a few people get that motivated for a few months, or even a year or two. Their sales volumes and commissions were impressive, but they still eventually quit the business. I feel that one big reason why they quit is that that type of hyped-up selling was their only impression of sales. They never realized that they could succeed without being in high gear all the time. They simply burned themselves out.

It has been said, "It is better to burn out than rust out." Maybe so, but if you are out, what is the difference? If you run constantly at full throttle, you will probably burn out; if you do not work hard enough, you will probably rust out. What better way than hourly selling to keep yourself at the most efficient cruising speed!

Living a balanced life is also important. Balancing your time between work, family and leisure is important to feeling comfortable with your career. Hourly selling keeps you working hard enough to be successful, but gives you enough time off for other aspects of your life.

It has occurred to me that even some of the *good* salespeople could use hourly selling to keep them from selling too much. They can get so wrapped up in success that they never stop to smell the roses. Many marriages and families have been strained because of that workaholic life style, to say nothing about the health effects of working so much without proper exercise and time off.

I have seen salespeople quit the business because of pressure from their spouses or fiancées. They failed to show them that sales can be handled much like a regular job.

It is often said that if you are in sales, you need an extremely understanding spouse. Understanding in what regard? It is usually suggested that your spouse must be willing to put up with your unusual and long hours. In other words, if your mate is not willing to let you be "gone selling" all the time, he or she is not understanding. I have never agreed with the logic in that, and I have doubts about the kind of relationship you would have with someone who thought it was fine for you to be gone all the time.

Of course, you need support from your spouse, and he or she must understand that you have to work hard and that your schedule will sometimes vary. Regardless of how ambitious you are, hourly selling will help you keep a predictable balance between work time and personal time. Furthermore, your spouse is more likely to be supportive if he or she knows that there is a predetermined limit to your work time each week. With hourly selling, you can even choose when to put your time in, which can aid in arriving at a mutually acceptable schedule.

Some salespeople in our business feel that they

have to go on the road for a few days at a time with a group of other salespeople to do their best. I certainly agree that that is an exciting way to get sales. However, to do that almost completely ignores your personal life. They say that they do it to be able to discipline their time more easily. All they really need to do is commit themselves to an hourly selling program right in their home area.

When I get my hours in for the week, *I am done.* I forget business. That way I am fresh and recharged Monday morning. I really like my business, but I try to maintain a "detached concern" for it.

As psychologist Albert Lipp says, "Hourly selling is psychologically sound because it is built around the individual salesperson." Since I know that hourly selling allows me to stay within my psychological comfort zone, I never dread going to work. A person is much more likely to remain in a job that he feels comfortable with.

10

Competition
and Association

After discovering how the hourly selling concept affects your ability to motivate yourself to sell, will you lose the need to compete and associate with other salespeople? Yes, you probably will. The fundamental principle of *Hourly Selling* is that all you really need is your sample kit and a car. You do not need a sales meeting or a contest of any kind to get you motivated to go selling. Your hourly goal will get you out there, and the resulting sales will keep you naturally motivated. For many years I felt I had to be around some other positive salespeople before I could get motivated to sell. It is not healthy to use other salespeople or a trophy as crutches to get you motivated because it implies that you will fail without them. The more you go after being number one, or the more you depend on everyone's recognition, the shallower your motivation. It becomes surface motivation that can go away as soon as its incentives are removed. Real, lasting motivation comes from within a person. It is there in the decision to enter a business and really want the independence and profit it provides. It is there in the willingness to pay the necessary price to make it work. Hourly selling clearly defines the amount of that price in a precalculated amount of effort each week.

The positive aspects of competition are obvious. The big advantage is that it provides a goal for salespeople. The idea of being number one or winning a contest can be quite exciting.

However, there are still some drawbacks to awards. If you are the kind of person who thinks you have to be number one at everything you do, you can become quite frustrated. If you kill yourself trying to beat the number-one salesperson but don't quite do it, you may burn yourself out. To be devastated if you are not number one is a ridiculous burden to saddle yourself with. In sales, as in sports, there will always eventually be someone better than you.

It may sound like I am advocating no sales meetings or competition. On the contrary, what I am advocating is a different perspective, which you will develop when you begin to use hourly selling. You will begin to look at association with other salespeople as an enjoyable side benefit of your job.

Instead of needing a positive sales meeting to motivate you, you will be one of the people making it positive. Winning a contest or a trophy will be an exciting bonus to what was originally a basic commitment just to do a job.

Consider a professional athlete. No one sees the days and years of work and sweat he puts out to being a pro. When the big day of his victory arrives, he receives a well-deserved reward, but he must first love the sport enough to enjoy playing it each and every day.

How about competition? As long as we are on the subject, let's see what hourly selling can do. If your real goal is to move up the ladder and beat someone else's totals, you should commit yourself to a high hourly goal. *Hourly Selling* produces a merciless, grinding consistency that only the very top producers can keep up with. You will virtually work your competition to death. They may get ahead of you for a while, but they will tire and perhaps even burn out in the long run. To you, it will all be just in a day's work. You will be just as fresh six months later as you were on the day you started.

If there is a contest, or if my sales are close to beating someone else's, I will not work one extra minute to try to be the winner. That may sound like an indifferent or lazy attitude, but you must remember that I have already set my hours. To be sure, they were based on an ambitious business goal, but all other aspects of my life were also taken into consideration. Allowing outside circumstances to raise or lower my selling hours destroys the whole idea of hourly selling. There will always be another contest offered or someone else to try to beat. My hours were set because of my goals, not someone else's. What good is it to win the battle but to lose the war? I want to win the war by having a successful sales career. However, I have been pleasantly surprised by the number of people I have outsold by using hourly selling. Not only is it satisfying to sell more than others, but it is nice to know I am doing it as a side benefit of setting my own goals. It is a measure of how much more disciplined my time is than theirs. As for the ones who are outselling me, I wonder if their lives are as balanced as mine. Don't get me wrong, I will always be seeking ways to improve my sales, but it will always be done within a controllable time structure.

It is fair to question why I go so much against the grain of traditional sales motivation. When I say that I refuse to compete or be affected by contests and awards and instead advocate very little enthusiasm and few goals or ambitions, you could understandably become suspicious. You may even conclude that I am certifiably insane. I do it, however, to emphasize the importance of internalizing your goals and motivation. By nature, many of us in sales are quite competitive and are easily swept into challenges and competition.

Before I began to use hourly selling I was probably one of the most susceptible. Whether it was personal sales or group sales, I would work myself to death trying to outdo others. I did earn lots of money, and I will admit that some competition is healthy. I would work sixty to eighty hours per week to accomplish my goals. I was willing to put out whatever effort was necessary.

I suppose there is something to be admired in that kind of ambition, but it also leaves a lot to be desired. When you are on a selling "high," it is hard to imagine needing anything or anyone else. A good sales organization will have lots of camaraderie among its salespeople, but this can easily become overused. When I and my sales crew were at our highest points, we worked and partied together. Sales is a tough business, and only another sales-person can really appreciate and respect what it takes to succeed. If one of us had a bad day, he *needed* to associate with the other salespeople. If he had a good day, he *wanted* to associate with the others. Whatever the case, our business and social lives became almost one and the same. This "social" form of motivation can be productive, and many sales companies use if very effectively.

The catch is that it ignores the fact that some salespeople may want to keep their personal or family lives separate from the sales business. It is not because they have a bad attitude towards their job; they just want to treat it more like a regular job. There is nothing wrong with that, and in the long run it is probably a more stable attitude anyway.

In my case, as the years wore on, I slowly,

surely, though subconsciously, was beginning to burn out. By the age of twenty-six, I had achieved more financial and business success than I had ever dreamed of, but it had been done at the expense of any substantial personal life. I craved being able to just be myself and take time off free of a business conversation.

As that craving turned into actions, my work schedule went to the opposite extreme. From the workaholic eighty-hour week, I slid down to barely a twenty-five-hour work week. My income dropped, and my self-esteem became confused. This kind of overcompensation is one of the biggest dangers of being overmotivated. So much motivational advice around today deals with "reaching your potential." This is off base because it too often promotes "*working* to your potential" rather than "*living* to your potential." "*Living* to your potential" in direct sales necessarily requires a way to discipline yourself to work hard enough to be successful, but it also means that you should not allow your business to control your entire life.

After drifting at a twenty-five-hour-per-week pace for a year or so, I tried to reestablish my goals and income. This was particularly difficult, because I still had not developed an hourly system. Out of a frustrated desire to be more successful, I made unwise financial moves that eventually led to my business crisis.

I could then also see how I had neglected my personal life. I had ignored my family and marriage,

I was overweight, and I was eating and drinking too much. I was just plain out of shape, both physically and mentally. All of this occurred simply because I was living such an unbalanced life.

I have seen other salespeople I know let similar things happen to themselves. One of the most extreme examples that comes to mind is a fellow from one of Royal Prestige's other franchise distributors that I got to know at national conventions. He was a real competitor who carried with him lots of excitement and enthusiasm. He was always the life of the party. I remember at one convention he was expecially excited. He was jumping around celebrating and making fun of jobs that were not in sales. I realize that salespeople are special and that we should be proud of our profession, but I deplore putting other people down. I must, however, regretfully admit that I used to do it too. Anyway, he had just won a number-one trophy for our summer contest, and he had worked very hard to get it. When he went up to accept his trophy at the awards banquet, he literally ran across the tops of a couple of tables on his way. Everybody was quite entertained by this fireball of a competitor!

It was only a few months later that I saw him again at a management seminar. He sat at the table with a blank look on his face, and he barely responded as ideas were exchanged. A couple of months later I discovered that he had quit the business. It is not necessary for us to speculate on what specific things made him quit. We can easily see that he was vulnerable to a number of pitfalls. The fact is that he quit.

What a shame. What a waste of the sales talent that he obviously had. Many salespeople make similar mistakes to some extent. It all can be avoided by using an hourly system.

Remember, I use hourly selling too. In fact, I used it for a long time before I put it into book form for other people. I know how competitive I can be, and I know the possible consequences. I now save my competitiveness for the racquetball court. Sales is no longer a game to me. It is a business, and a business should be run as rationally as possible. Because of this, I will change my time structure only for business or personal reasons, and not because a contest has been plopped on me.

One amusing side effect of going on hourly selling is that it starts to self-destruct, but then saves itself by its own definition. Let me explain: If your selling time has been undisciplined and you decide to use hourly selling, your sales volume will almost certainly increase. By definition, your goal changes from getting sales to just putting hours in. You no longer care if you get sales when you start to work, which makes you more relaxed. Just as you really get into the idea of relaxed selling, you start to get more sales, which is of course exciting. More importantly, you will probably start to outsell people that you have never outsold before. This causes you to enjoy competition again, which leads you to want to sell more so you can outsell still more people.

The result is that you again want to make sales when you start to work. Then, just as you start feeling uptight about getting more and more sales, you say "Stop! Wait a minute!" These extra sales are great, and it is nice to outsell some people, but that is not your *primary* goal; it is only a benefit of hourly selling. So you again remind yourself not to care so much about sales and just to concentrate on getting your hours in. Hourly selling is a comforting concept to return to whenever you find yourself getting uptight about wanting sales, regardless of what is causing you to feel that way.

If competition is a true goal for you, hourly selling can still be used. Say, for example, you are in a four-week contest: You can increase your quota of hours for those weeks. Based on your weekly volume per hour, you can get a pretty accurate estimate of the number of hours that will be needed. Furthermore, hourly selling will make your schedule more predictable during the contest period.

Regardless of your specific goals, hourly selling is a tangible framework you can use to realize your specific goals, no matter what they are.

11

Comparisons
of Hourly Selling

Let us review how you sell hourly. You have arrived at a certain number of hours that you will spend on selling during each week, and you have a list of selling activities that you may use to fill those hours. The rule is that you must always be doing one of the selling activities. You may slow down or speed up your pace as your mood dictates, but to count the time as selling time, you must always be doing one of the selling activities. It can be an activity as casual as sitting and organizing your leads or as ambitious as cold canvassing. You can also switch from one activity to another anytime you wish to do so. There are two provisions for driving time: If you are going from one area to another you can drive up to fifteen minutes and count all of that time as selling time; if you are driving to a preset sales appointment, you may drive up to one hour and count all of that time as selling time.

Once your hours are set and your selling activities are established, getting your hours in becomes your one and only goal for the week. It does not matter if you are in a positive or a negative mood or if you are enthused or not; much of the needed enthusiasm is generated as you get involved in the selling activities. When I am not getting the sales I want and am feeling low, I do not need a positive sales meeting. What I really need is sales! What better way to solve the problem than by continuing to fill my time with activities that will eventually result in sales?

Imagine that you have a tiny time clock that you carry with you all week long. When you begin selling, you start the clock. The clock runs for as long as you stay within the guidelines of selling time. If you stop selling for a while, you stop the clock until you resume selling. You just have to be sure that by the end of the week your time clock has been running for a total of what your preset hours are.

You have ultimate control of when and where to sell as long as your time clock is kept running. For example, you may have some office work to do. If you have forty-five minutes to spare, you may leave and go selling for that time so that you can start your selling-time clock, thus making the end of your week that much closer. One misconception is that if you do not have the time to put on a sales call, it is not worth the effort to go out and sell. If you really give hourly selling a chance, you will discover that many good things can be accomplished during these short selling periods. Many times I dig up good leads or line up appointments that I would never have contacted if I had not put that time in. Let us say that, for the moment, you are so unmotivated that you cannot even remain within the hourly selling guidelines. Fine. Just stop entirely. Of course, your time clock stops as well. Just remember that any time taken off must be made up by the end of the week. It is comforting to know that at any given time you can quit completely and not even feel guilty about it. Maybe there is an event you want to attend. Whether it is a ball game, a personal or family event, or just a television program, you can go and not be tortured with guilt. The catch is that the lost time will have to be made up that week unless you declare some vacation time. That is why you do not have to feel guilty. You are not cheating on your time, you are just rearranging it. One good thing about hourly selling is that it makes you scrutinize which events are worth rearranging your time for. It is also somehow easier to stay out working when you know that you can quit if you really want to. On the other hand, hourly selling rewards you if you happen to work longer than you planned on a given day. If I give lots of demonstrations on a long day, I become tired but never bitter. How many families have been strained because the salesperson is "always gone selling?" In sales, it is hard to avoid working some long days, but my family and

I know it means I will have fewer hours of work during the remainder of the week. If a salesperson's family is not bitter for those reasons, they are more likely to give important positive support.

Hourly selling is a way of pacing yourself in a business where much is left to your judgement. If you are able to vary your pace and choose from a variety of selling activities, you will feel like you have worked, but you will seldom feel exhausted or burnt out. The same effect occurs when you work those short periods of selling time in between other priorities in your day. If you have the impression that your work is rather effortless, you do not dread it as much. Furthermore, stress will become less of a factor because you will become accustomed to just getting your hours in rather than making sales. You will learn to take a bad week in stride because you know the sales will eventually average out with your hours.

Many times a salesperson's attitude or effort is judged by his sales in a given week. Not with hourly selling. Sometimes, after I have had a very good week, someone will say to me, "You sure must have been motivated and worked hard this week." Nope, not me. With hourly selling, my effort is exactly the same each week. My good weeks occur when the sales just happen to come. Of course, after rather poor weeks of sales, people will say to me, "You must have been unmotivated and lazy." Well, I am on hourly selling, so don't ever insult me by thinking that I cheated on my time. My efforts just did not happen to pay off very well that week.

To be sure, hourly selling involves a certain amount of drudgery. The most obvious example of this is the constant keeping track of your selling time and interruptions. However, that becomes more second nature and routine as time goes by. Re-copying and organizing your leads can also be drudgery or at least low-level, unchallenging activity. Even putting on presentations can become routine, especially if you start giving more of them. Worst of all is having to push yourself to keep going when you have no appointments set up and you are already tired. There is also a certain amount of relatively inactive time involved whenever you are driving.

I do not like that feeling of drudgery either, but few professions are without it. A factory worker's job might be more routine than an executive's job, but many executives can tell you how weary they become of reading reports and signing forms.

It is somewhat comforting to know that most jobs have drudgery, and furthermore, I think sales even needs some. Remember earlier when I talked about how exciting it was that I had managed to make selling seem boring? If you are pushing yourself to continue and are tired, you probably are feeling the effects of your hourly commitment from a physical perspective, and that is good. Few great things are accomplished without some hard work.

Your "down time" while selling can be used to daydream about your favorite hobby or just to have some time to yourself for thought and reflection. I put together most of the ideas for this book while

I was out selling. When I finally sat down to write, I knew exactly what I wanted to say. Any routineness that hourly selling produces can be used creatively and contributes to the feeling of having a "normal job."

Hourly selling amounts to constantly doing something for today, tomorrow, and the future. When I am working I naturally hope for an immediate sale, but I am also content to know that my efforts may pay off in a day or two or even farther in the future. That is what makes sales so consistent with hourly selling. Anyone can get hot and have a big week. When an *average* salesperson of that second category has a good week, he probably was only cashing in on some good leads. He neglects to put extra time in accumulating more leads for future weeks. If an *average* salesperson has a big week, it is usually followed by a couple of very poor weeks, thus making his overall average quite mediocre. A person using hourly selling invariably has a better stock of leads than an *average* salesperson because he constantly does things that produce and weed out his leads. If you are a *good* salesperson, you have a reasonable chance of outselling me for the year. However, you had better be prepared to work all week, every week, all year, or my consistency will grind you to death.

In a year's period of time, there are many things that can happen to you that may affect your attitude. Everyone in the human race has occasional problems, either personal or business. It is nice to have a selling system that does not depend on your attitude. You become a sort of emotionless selling machine that plops itself out onto the selling field for a preset number of hours each week. You personally may still be bothered by your problems, but your effort will not be. I have seen salespeople use a problem as an excuse not to go out selling. They say, for example, that if they are in a bad mood they will not be very effective when selling. Maybe so, but a salesperson out selling while in a bad mood is still more effective than a salesperson sitting at home while in a bad mood. Hourly selling is a way to proceed as though nothing is wrong. Furthermore, sometimes getting out to sell will improve your mood or help you to forget a problem for a while. In this situation, I would probably start with some low-level selling activity such as searching for leads or confirming orders with previous customers. You pace yourself by shifting gears from time to time. This also creates more variety in your job. Time is life, and we all have a limited amount of it. Hourly selling is a way of keeping track of your business life while keeping in tune with your personal time.

If my hourly selling ideas are criticized, I can always fall back on the fact that they work! I challenge you to try hourly selling for a few weeks and see if you don't get results as well as extra peace of mind. I have even had fun trying to make it *not* work at times. I have tried just barely staying within the guidelines by lazily staying with very low-level selling, but I have literally stumbled across sales despite myself. I have had those bad mood days, too. I can document times that I have gotten sales simply because I was out working. Keep in mind that hourly selling assumes that you are reasonably well-trained and experienced, so you therefore know what to do when you finally get in front of a good prospect.

Anyone who analyzes how I so drastically improved my sales with hourly selling could say that all I did was to start spending more time selling. That would be true, but it would be an oversimplification. The key is that hourly selling is the only way I ever discovered to discipline myself to put in that extra selling time. Hourly selling works because it represents an accumulation of both my own experience and that of numerous other salespeople I have worked with over many years. I am putting hourly selling into book form because I believe it can really help many other salespeople. Regardless of our specific businesses, we are all vulnerable to many of the same pitfalls of sales. However, we are also exposed to the same opportunities that sales provides. To use hourly selling successfully, you simply have to be willing to use it in its entirety. It is my hope that your experience so far in sales, along with my book, will convince you that an hourly selling approach to sales is the only way to assure yourself of consistent sales and a balanced life.

Compare your direct-sales job to owning a retail store. In a large sense, direct sales is being in business for yourself. Direct sales, like retail sales, depends on what I refer to as the "high-traffic idea." If you own a retail store, not everyone that walks by will stop in and look around. Not everyone who stops in will buy something. However, you will remain in business for as long as people buy enough to make your store profitable. You are not especially upset by the people who do not buy, because you are still making a profit. If your store is open for enough hours, enough people will stop in and purchase something. In direct sales, you are the store and you are open only when you are putting in selling time. How many hours per week will you be "open for business?"...!

12

Getting Started

Getting started begins with a commitment from yourself—a commitment to improve your sales, live a more balanced life, or both. After making the decision to go on an hourly selling system, you must tailor the system to your specific sales job.

The selling activities that I talked about apply to most sales jobs, but there will obviously be some differences from job to job. Spend some time observing and analyzing your business. Start at the end and think backwards. In other words, take your sales, which are the desired result, and analyze where they come from. What are all the activities that contribute to your sales? Observe your own sales in your business, as well as anyone else's. You should come up with a list of selling activities fairly similar to my list in Chapter 6.

Second, try to calculate how many hours you have actually been working each week. This will be helpful in making decisions on future improvements. By gathering just a few facts, you may already be able to come up with an approximate hourly volume for your past sales. That can be exciting when making a commitment to set your hours.

Above all, start realistically. If you discover that you have actually been putting in only twenty productive hours per week, do not bump it up to forty the first week you use hourly selling. Maybe start with twenty-five hours for a couple of weeks. Then, as you get accustomed to the whole idea, gradually increase your hours to your desired level. Look at it as going to your boss and asking if you can work more hours because you need the money. Since you are your own boss, you always say "sure." Just be prepared for the shock of how hard it is to get your hours in each week, regardless of circumstances.

The rest of the "how-to's" of hourly selling have already been covered in previous chapters, which you may occasionally want to refer back to.

Hourly selling is as simple as verifying the list of selling activities in your business, setting your hours, and then following the hourly selling guidelines.

The number of hours you set will depend completely on you. Is your job part-time or full-time? Do you have management responsibilities? Most importantly, what are your business and personal goals?

It requires some imagination to use the hourly selling idea, but the power of the human mind is unlimited. If you can believe in an idea or concept, you can make it work. We become what we think about all day long. To be independent is not to be without a boss, but rather to be your own boss. This method provides you with some guidelines on how to be your own boss. You still have ultimate control of when and how much to work. Now, however, you must justify every change ahead of time. If you picture yourself as a *good* salesperson with a foolproof method of disciplining your time, you may actually become a *good* salesperson!

A Library of Prentice-Hall Books on Selling

Bettger, Frank. *How I Multiplied My Income and Happiness in Selling.* (1982)

Bettger, Frank. *How I Raised Myself from Failure to Success in Selling.* (1982)

Gold, Carol S. *Solid Gold Customer Relations: A Professional Resource Guide.* (1983)

Goodman, Gary. *Reach Out and Sell Someone: How to Phone Your Way to Profit and Success Through the Goodman System of Telemarketing.* (1983)

Goodman, Gary. *Winning by Telephone: Telephone Effectiveness for the Businessman and Consumer.* (1983)

Horvath, Walter. *How to Use Your Selling Power.* (1982)

Montgomery, Robert L. *How to Sell in the 1980's: Successful Selling of Products, Services, and Ideas in a New Decade* (1980)

Patton, Forrest H. *The Psychology of Closing Sales.* (1984)

Pesce, Vince. *A Complete Manual of Professional Selling: The Modular Approach to Sales and Success.* (1983)

Stern, Francis M., and Ron Zemke. *Stressless Selling: A Guide to Success for Men and Women in Sales.* (1981)

Wheeler, Elmer. *Sizzlemanship.* (1983)

Wichert, Jack. *How to be a Successful Salesperson.* (1984)

Wilbur, L. Perry. *On Your Way to the Top in Selling.* (1983)

Index